DRUG TRANSIT AND DISTRIBUTION, INTERCEPTION AND CONTROL

MARIJUANA

EMERGING LEGAL ISSUES AND FEDERAL TAX PROPOSALS

DRUG TRANSIT AND DISTRIBUTION, INTERCEPTION AND CONTROL

Additional books in this series can be found on Nova's website under the Series tab.

Additional e-books in this series can be found on Nova's website under the e-book tab.

DRUG TRANSIT AND DISTRIBUTION, INTERCEPTION AND CONTROL

MARIJUANA

EMERGING LEGAL ISSUES AND FEDERAL TAX PROPOSALS

VICTOR P. TYSON
EDITOR

nova publishers
New York

Library of Congress Cataloging-in-Publication Data

ISBN: 978-1-63482-057-8

Published by Nova Science Publishers, Inc. † New York

CONTENTS

PREFACE

This book analyzes some legal issues related to marijuana and provides some proposals to resolve the issues. It also discusses federal tax proposals for marijuana.

Chapter 1 - The federal Controlled Substances Act (CSA) outlaws the possession, cultivation, or distribution of marijuana except for authorized research. Twenty states have regulatory schemes that allow possession, cultivation, or distribution of marijuana for medicinal purposes. Two have revenue regimes that allow possession, cultivation, or sale generally. The U.S. Constitution's Supremacy Clause preempts any state law that conflicts with federal law. Although there is some division, the majority of state courts have concluded that the federal-state marijuana law conflict does not require preemption of state medical marijuana laws. The legal consequences of a CSA violation, however, remain in place. Nevertheless, current federal criminal enforcement guidelines counsel confining investigations and prosecutions to the most egregious affront to federal interests.

Legal and ethical considerations limit the extent to which an attorney may advise and assist a client intent on participating in his or her state's medical or recreational marijuana system. Bar associations differ on the precise boundaries of those limitations.

State medical marijuana laws grant registered patients, their doctors, and providers immunity from the consequences of state law. The Washington and Colorado retail marijuana regimes authorize the commercial exploitation of the marijuana market in small taxable doses.

The present and potential consequences of a CSA violation can be substantial. Cultivation or sale of marijuana on all but the smallest scale invites a five-year mandatory minimum prison term. Revenues and the property used to generate them may merely be awaiting federal collection under federal forfeiture laws. Federal tax laws deny marijuana entrepreneurs the benefits available to other businesses. Banks may afford marijuana merchants financial services only if the bank files a suspicious activity report (SAR) for every marijuana-related transaction, and only if it conducts a level of due diligence into its customers' activities sufficient to unearth any affront to federal interests.

Marijuana users may not possess a firearm or ammunition. They may not hold federal security clearances. They may not operate commercial trucks, buses, trains, or planes. Federal contractors and private employers may be free to refuse to hire them and to fire them. If fired, they may be ineligible for unemployment compensation. They may be denied federally assisted housing.

At the heart of the federal-state conflict lies a disagreement over dangers and benefits inherent in marijuana use. The CSA authorizes research on controlled substances, including those in Schedule I such as marijuana, that may address those questions. Members have introduced a number of bills in the 113th Congress that speak to the conflict. Only the proposals found in the farm bill (P.L. 113-79 (H.R. 2642)) have been enacted thus far.

Chapter 2 - The combination of state policy and general public opinion favoring the legalizing of marijuana has led some in Congress to advocate for legalization and taxation of marijuana at the federal level. The Marijuana Tax Equity Act of 2013 (H.R. 501) would impose a federal excise tax of 50% on the producer and importer price of marijuana. The National Commission on Federal Marijuana Policy Act of 2013 (H.R. 1635) proposes establishing a National Commission on Federal Marijuana Policy that would review the potential revenue generated by taxing marijuana, among other things.

This report focuses solely on issues surrounding a potential federal marijuana tax. First, it provides a brief overview of marijuana production. Second, it presents possible justifications for taxes and, in some cases, estimates the level of tax suggested by that rationale. Third, it analyzes possible marijuana tax designs. The report also discusses various tax administration and enforcement issues, such as labeling and tracking.

Economic theory suggests the efficient level of taxation is equal to marijuana's external cost to society. Studies conducted in the United Kingdom (UK) and Canada suggest that the costs of individual marijuana consumption to society are between 12% and 28% of the costs of an individual alcohol user, and total social costs are even lower after accounting for the smaller number of marijuana users in society. Based on an economic estimate of $30 billion of net external costs for alcohol, the result is an external cost of $0.5 billion to

$1.6 billion annually for marijuana. These calculations imply that an upper limit to the economically efficient tax rate could be $0.30 per marijuana cigarette (containing an average of one half of a gram of marijuana) or $16.80 per ounce. An increased number of users in a legal market would raise total costs, but not necessarily costs per unit.

Some could also view excise taxes as a means to curtail demand, particularly as the price of marijuana can be expected to drop from current retail prices of up $200-$300 per ounce to prices closer to the cost of production at $5-$18 per ounce, if broadly legalized. The demand for marijuana is estimated to be relatively price inelastic, meaning that consumer demand is relatively insensitive to price changes. Although previous studies of marijuana demand largely examine consumers willing to engage in illegal activities, it appears that higher tax rates would have a minor effect on reducing demand. With this said, tax policy, coupled with adequate law enforcement, could be an effective tool to limit marijuana consumption among youth, as empirical studies indicate that their demand is more sensitive to price than non-youth.

Excise taxes on marijuana could also be levied primarily to raise revenue, as has been historically the case with tobacco and alcohol. As an illustration, assuming a total market size of $40 billion, a federal tax of $50 per ounce is estimated to raise about $6.8 billion annually, after accounting for behavioral effects associated with price decreases following legalization.

The choices in administrative design could affect consumer behavior, production methods, evasion rates, or the tax base of a federal marijuana excise tax. Some of the more significant choices include whether to exempt medicinal uses or homegrown marijuana from tax.

In: Marijuana
Editor: Victor P. Tyson

ISBN: 978-1-63482-057-8

Chapter 1

MARIJUANA: MEDICAL AND RETAIL—SELECTED LEGAL ISSUES*

Todd Garvey and Charles Doyle

SUMMARY

The federal Controlled Substances Act (CSA) outlaws the possession, cultivation, or distribution of marijuana except for authorized research. Twenty states have regulatory schemes that allow possession, cultivation, or distribution of marijuana for medicinal purposes. Two have revenue regimes that allow possession, cultivation, or sale generally. The U.S. Constitution's Supremacy Clause preempts any state law that conflicts with federal law. Although there is some division, the majority of state courts have concluded that the federal-state marijuana law conflict does not require preemption of state medical marijuana laws. The legal consequences of a CSA violation, however, remain in place. Nevertheless, current federal criminal enforcement guidelines counsel confining investigations and prosecutions to the most egregious affront to federal interests.

Legal and ethical considerations limit the extent to which an attorney may advise and assist a client intent on participating in his or her state's medical or recreational marijuana system. Bar associations differ on the precise boundaries of those limitations.

* This is an edited, reformatted and augmented version of a Congressional Research Service publication R43435, prepared for Members and Committees of Congress dated March 25, 2014.

State medical marijuana laws grant registered patients, their doctors, and providers immunity from the consequences of state law. The Washington and Colorado retail marijuana regimes authorize the commercial exploitation of the marijuana market in small taxable doses.

The present and potential consequences of a CSA violation can be substantial. Cultivation or sale of marijuana on all but the smallest scale invites a five-year mandatory minimum prison term. Revenues and the property used to generate them may merely be awaiting federal collection under federal forfeiture laws. Federal tax laws deny marijuana entrepreneurs the benefits available to other businesses. Banks may afford marijuana merchants financial services only if the bank files a suspicious activity report (SAR) for every marijuana-related transaction, and only if it conducts a level of due diligence into its customers' activities sufficient to unearth any affront to federal interests.

Marijuana users may not possess a firearm or ammunition. They may not hold federal security clearances. They may not operate commercial trucks, buses, trains, or planes. Federal contractors and private employers may be free to refuse to hire them and to fire them. If fired, they may be ineligible for unemployment compensation. They may be denied federally assisted housing.

At the heart of the federal-state conflict lies a disagreement over dangers and benefits inherent in marijuana use. The CSA authorizes research on controlled substances, including those in Schedule I such as marijuana, that may address those questions. Members have introduced a number of bills in the 113th Congress that speak to the conflict. Only the proposals found in the farm bill (P.L. 113-79 (H.R. 2642)) have been enacted thus far.

INTRODUCTION

Federal law classifies marijuana as a Schedule I Controlled Substance.[1] As a result, it is a federal crime to grow, sell, or merely possess the drug. In addition to facing the prospect of a federal criminal prosecution, those who violate the federal Controlled Substances Act (CSA) may suffer a number of additional adverse consequences under federal law. For example, federal authorities may confiscate any property used to grow marijuana or facilitate its sale or use; marijuana users may lose their jobs, their homes, or their right to possess a firearm or ammunition; and sellers of marijuana may lose the tax benefits and banking services that other merchants enjoy, and ultimately their businesses.

Nevertheless, without federal statutory sanction, 20 states have established medical marijuana regulatory regimes. Two have gone further and "legalized" marijuana under state recreational marijuana laws.[2] State officials lack the constitutional authority necessary to trump conflicting federal law. Federal officials, however, lack the unlimited resources necessary to trump the impact of conflicting state law.

The following is an analysis of some of the legal issues the situation has generated and some of the proposals to resolve them.

BACKGROUND

Federal regulation of the drugs, chemicals, and plants now considered controlled substances began with the Harrison Narcotics Act of 1914.[3] Relying upon its constitutional power to tax, commerce power, and power to implement the nation's treaty obligations,[4] Congress used the legislation to establish a system under which it taxed lawful medicinal use and proscribed abuse.[5]

Little more than two decades later, Congress supplemented the Harrison Act with the Marihuana Tax Act of 1937,[6] explicitly noting reliance on its tax, commerce, and territorial powers.[7] The Marihuana Act replicated the Harrison Act's procedures in large measure[8] and adopted by cross-reference the Harrison Act's penalty structure.[9] It became apparent over time, however, that the Marihuana Act served no real revenue purpose and in fact had "become, in effect, solely a criminal law imposing sanctions upon persons who [sold], acquire[d], or possess[ed] marihuana."[10]

This proved problematic when the Supreme Court pointed out the Fifth Amendment difficulties inherent in a tax-based enforcement structure like that of the Harrison and Marihuana Tax Acts. The Court in *Marchetti* observed that a gambler's "obligations to register and to pay the [federal] occupational tax created ... real and appreciable ... hazards of self-incrimination" under federal and state anti-gambling laws.[11] The same day, in *Haynes,* it held that by the same token "the constitutional privilege against self-incrimination provides a full defense to prosecutions either for failure to register a firearm ... or for possession of an unregistered firearm" under the tax-based structure of the National Firearms Act.[12] Finally, in *Leahy*, it struck closer to home. There, it held that the Fifth Amendment privilege against self-incrimination provided a full defense to a charge of transporting marijuana acquired without paying the Marihuana Tax Act transfer tax.[13]

Within months, the Senate Judiciary Committee reported out a Commerce Clause/treaty-based controlled substances proposal that featured most of the components ultimately found in the Controlled Substances Act.[14] It classified marijuana with the most tightly regulated substances in Schedule I, but punished its abuse less severely, explaining in its critique of an earlier proposal that

> [T]o impose the same high mandatory minimum penalties for marihuana-related offenses as for LSD and heroin offenses is inequitable in the face of a considerable amount of evidence that marihuana is significantly less harmful and dangerous than LSD or heroin.
>
> It had also become apparent that the severity of penalties including the length of sentences does not affect the extent of drug abuse and other drug-related violations. The basic consideration here was that the increasingly longer sentences that had been legislated in the past had not shown the expected overall reduction in drug law violations. The opposite had been true notably in the case of marihuana. Under Federal law and under many States laws marihuana violations carry the same strict penalties that are applicable to hard narcotics, yet marijuana violations have almost doubled in the last 2 years alone.
>
> In addition, the severe drug laws specifically as applied to marihuana have helped create a serious clash between segments of the youth generation and the Government. These youths consider the marihuana laws hypocritical and unjust. Because of these laws the marihuana issue has contributed to the broader problem of alienation of youth from the general society and to a general feeling of disrespect for the law and judicial process.[15]

Consistent with this view, it called for the establishment of a study commission to examine and make recommendations on the troubling marijuana-related issues.[16] The Commission's final report recommended the legalization of possession of marijuana for private personal use, but that the Controlled Substance Act otherwise remain unchanged.[17]

Controlled Substances Act Today

Congress enacted the Controlled Substances Act (CSA)[18] as Title II of the Comprehensive Drug Abuse Prevention and Control Act of 1970.[19] The purpose of the CSA is to regulate and facilitate the manufacture, distribution, and use of controlled substances for legitimate medical, scientific, research, and industrial purposes, and to prevent these substances from being diverted for illegal purposes. The CSA places various plants, drugs, and chemicals (such as narcotics, stimulants, depressants, hallucinogens, and anabolic steroids) into one of five schedules based on the substance's medical use, potential for abuse, and safety or dependence liability.[20]

Schedule I substances are deemed to have no currently accepted medical use in treatment and can be used only in very limited circumstances, whereas substances classified in Schedules II, III, IV, and V have recognized medical uses and may be manufactured, distributed, and used in accordance with the CSA. The CSA requires persons who handle controlled substances (such as drug manufacturers, wholesale distributors, doctors, hospitals, pharmacies, and scientific researchers) to register with the Drug Enforcement Administration (DEA) in the U.S. Department of Justice, the federal agency that administers and enforces the CSA.[21] Such registrants are subject to strict requirements regarding drug security, recordkeeping, reporting, and maintaining production quotas, in order to minimize theft and diversion.[22]

Because controlled substances classified as Schedule I drugs have "a high potential for abuse" with "no currently accepted medical use in treatment in the United States" and lack "accepted safety for use of the drug [] under medical supervisions,"[23] they may not be dispensed under a prescription, and such substances may be used only for bona fide, federal government-approved research studies.[24] Under the CSA, only doctors licensed by the Drug Enforcement Administration (DEA) are allowed to prescribe controlled substances listed in Schedules II-V to patients.[25] Federal regulations stipulate that a lawful prescription for a controlled substance may be issued only "for a legitimate medical purpose by an individual practitioner acting in the usual course of his professional practice."[26]

The CSA establishes an administrative mechanism for substances to be controlled (added to a schedule); decontrolled (removed from the scheduling framework altogether); and rescheduled or transferred from one schedule to another.[27] Federal rulemaking proceedings to add, delete, or change the schedule of a drug or substance may be initiated by the DEA, the U.S. Department of Health and Human Services (HHS), or by petition by any interested person.[28] Petitions for rescheduling marijuana have been largely unsuccessful.[29] Congress may also change the scheduling status of a drug or substance through legislation.

Penalties777

Federal civil and criminal penalties are available for anyone who manufactures, distributes, imports, or possesses controlled substances in violation of the CSA (both "regulatory" offenses as well as illicit drug trafficking and possession).[30]

When Congress enacted the CSA in 1970, marijuana was classified as a Schedule I drug.[31] Today, marijuana is still categorized as a Schedule I controlled substance and is therefore subject to the most severe restrictions contained within the CSA. Pursuant to the CSA, the unauthorized cultivation, distribution, or possession of marijuana is a federal crime.[32] Although various factors contribute to the ultimate sentence received, the mere possession of marijuana generally constitutes a misdemeanor subject to up to one year imprisonment and a minimum fine of $1,000.[33] A violation of the federal "simple possession" statute that occurs after a single prior conviction under any federal or state drug law triggers a mandatory minimum fine of $2,500 and a minimum imprisonment term of 15 days (up to a maximum of two years); if the defendant has multiple prior drug offense convictions at the time of his or her federal simple possession offense, the sentencing court must impose a mandatory minimum fine of $5,000 and a mandatory minimum imprisonment term of 90 days (up to a maximum term of three years).[34] On the other hand, the cultivation or distribution of marijuana, or the possession of marijuana with the intent to distribute, is subject to more severe penalties, ranging from imprisonment for five years to imprisonment for life.[35] Moreover, property associated with the offense may be confiscated without or with any prior or accompanying criminal conviction.[36]

Forfeiture

Either in addition to, or in lieu of, bringing criminal prosecutions, the Department of Justice (DOJ) may choose to rely more heavily on the civil forfeiture provisions of the CSA in order to disrupt the operation of marijuana dispensaries and production facilities. Forfeiture is a penalty associated with a particular crime in which property is confiscated or otherwise divested from the owner and forfeited to the government, in accordance with constitutionally required due process procedures.[37]

Property forfeiture is used both to enforce criminal laws and to deter crime. Forfeitures are classified as civil or criminal depending on the nature of the judicial procedure which ends in confiscation. Civil forfeiture is ordinarily the product of a civil, *in rem* (against the property) proceeding in which the property is treated as the offender. No criminal charges are necessary against the owner, landlord, or mortgage holder because the guilt or innocence of the property owner, landlord, mortgage holder, or anyone else with a secured interest in the property is irrelevant; it is enough that the property was involved in, or otherwise connected to, an illegal activity (in which forfeiture is authorized).[38] Criminal forfeiture proceedings, on the other hand, are *in personam* (against the person) actions, and confiscation is possible only upon the conviction of the owner of the property and only to the extent of the defendant's interest in the property.[39] Property that is subject to forfeiture includes both the direct and indirect proceeds of illegal activities as well as any property used, or intended to be used, to facilitate that crime.[40]

Section 511 of the CSA (21 U.S.C. §881) makes a wide array of property associated with violations of the CSA subject to seizure by the Attorney General and forfeiture to the United States. Property subject to the CSA's civil forfeiture provision includes any controlled substance that has been manufactured, distributed, dispensed, acquired, or possessed in violation of federal law, as well as any equipment, firearm, money, mode of transportation, or real property *used or intended to be used to facilitate a violation of the CSA*.[41] In order to seize the covered property, the government need only show that the property is subject to forfeiture by a preponderance of the evidence.[42] Once forfeited, the Attorney General may destroy the controlled substances seized, and sell the other property at public auction.[43] After expenses of the forfeiture proceeding are recouped, excess funds are forwarded to the DOJ Asset Forfeiture Fund.[44]

Forfeiture proceedings are generally less resource intensive than a criminal prosecution and have been used in the past against medical marijuana dispensaries.[45] In practice, DOJ would be able to seize and liquidate property, both real and personal, associated with marijuana production, distribution, or retail sale facilities, without bringing any criminal action. As explained above, a civil asset forfeiture proceeding is a civil proceeding against the property in question. Although an interested party may object to the seizure, given that such facilities are in clear violation of federal law, so long as the property is indeed being used for marijuana-related activities, it would appear unlikely that many successful challenges to these actions could be waged.[46]

Developments in the States

Most of the states have legislation modeled after the federal Controlled Substances Act.[47] Over the years, some have reduced possession of small amounts of marijuana to a civil offense under state law.[48] Several have also created a state law exception for medical marijuana.[49] Colorado and Washington have enacted legislation authorizing the growth, sale, and possession of marijuana under state law.[50]

Medical Marijuana Laws

State medical marijuana laws follow a general pattern, although most have some individual characteristics and the manner in which they are enforced can differ considerably. Some of their features are attributable to the CSA and a case from the United States Court of Appeals for the Ninth Circuit, *Conant v. Walters.*[51]

Conant, a California physician, sought to enjoin the federal government from revoking his authority to prescribe controlled substances at all in retaliation for his recommending marijuana to some of his patients.[52] Then, as now, the CSA permits the Attorney General, acting through the Drug Enforcement Administration (DEA), to withdraw a physician's authority to prescribe controlled substances upon a failure to comply with the demands of the CSA.[53]

The Ninth Circuit acknowledged the prospect of criminal liability if the doctor were doing more than engaging in an abstract discussion with his patient: "A doctor would aid and abet by acting with the specific intent to provide a patient with the means to acquire marijuana. Similarly, a conspiracy would require that a doctor have knowledge that a patient intends to acquire marijuana, agree to help the patient acquire marijuana, and intend to help the patient acquire marijuana."[54] Yet, "[h]olding doctors responsible for whatever conduct the doctor could anticipate a patient *might* engage in after leaving the doctor's office is simply beyond the scope of either conspiracy or aiding and abetting."[55] On the other hand, such doctor-patient discussions do implicate First Amendment free speech principles. The Ninth Circuit therefore affirmed the district court's order which had enjoined any DEA enforcement action.[56]

As a consequence of the CSA and the *Conant* decision, the state medical marijuana laws are predicated upon a doctor's recommendation, rather than a prescription and the medicine is dispensed other than through a pharmacy.[57] In addition, the laws afford registered patients, care givers, cultivators, and distributors immunity from the consequences of state criminal laws.[58]

Patients

Physicians may recommend medical marijuana only for patients suffering from one or more statutorily defined "debilitating," or "qualifying" medical conditions. The typical list would include the following:

> "Debilitating medical condition" means one or more of the following:
>
> a) Cancer, glaucoma, positive status for human immunodeficiency virus, acquired immune deficiency syndrome, hepatitis c, amyotrophic lateral sclerosis, crohn's disease, agitation of alzheimer's disease or the treatment of these conditions.
> b) A chronic or debilitating disease or medical condition or its treatment that produces one or more of the following: cachexia or wasting syndrome; severe and chronic pain; severe nausea; seizures, including those characteristic of epilepsy; or severe and persistent muscle spasms, including those characteristic of multiple sclerosis.
> c) Any other medical condition or its treatment added by the department pursuant to section 36-2801.01.[59]

The list usually includes a condition such as "severe pain," or "chronic pain," or "severe and chronic pain" that is easy to claim, difficult to diagnose, and grounds for potential abuse. Some states seek to limit the scope of the term by statute or by regulation.[60] In many jurisdictions, a qualified patient must be a resident of the jurisdiction.[61] Most states and the District of Columbia restrict the amount of marijuana a patient may possess for medical purposes. The limit is usually an amount less than three ounces.[62] Medical marijuana statutes ordinarily do not allow patients to use marijuana in public.[63]

Caregivers

Caregivers must register and have been designated by one or more registered medical marijuana patients.[64] Medical marijuana laws afford caregivers the same immunity and impose the same limitations upon them as apply to patients.[65]

Dispensaries

Some state medical marijuana laws contemplate cultivation exclusively by the patient or his or her caregiver.[66] Most, however, establish a regulatory scheme for dispensaries.[67]

Retail Marijuana

Two states, Washington and Colorado, have established retail marijuana regimes. Both regulate the distribution of marijuana without a necessary medical nexus, but raise many of the same federal-state conflict issues found in the medical marijuana statutes.

Washington

Approved by a majority of Washington voters in November 2012, Washington Initiative 502 legalizes marijuana possession by amending state law to provide that the possession of small amounts of marijuana "is not a violation of this section, this chapter, or any other provision of Washington law."[68] Under the Initiative, individuals over the age of 21 may possess up to one ounce of dried marijuana, 16 ounces of marijuana infused product in solid form, or 72 ounces of marijuana infused product in liquid form.[69] However, marijuana must be used in private, as it is unlawful to "open a package containing marijuana ... or consume marijuana ... in view of the general public."[70]

In addition to legalizing possession, the Initiative provides that the "possession, delivery, distribution, and sale" by a validly licensed producer, processor, or retailer, in accordance with the newly established regulatory scheme administered by the state Liquor Control Board (LCB), "shall not be a criminal or civil offense under Washington state law."[71] The Initiative establishes a three-tiered production, processing, and retail licensing system that permits the state to retain regulatory control over the commercial life cycle of marijuana. Qualified individuals must obtain a producer's license to grow or cultivate marijuana, a processor's license to process, package, and label the drug, or a retail license to sell marijuana to the general public.[72]

The Initiative establishes various restrictions and requirements for obtaining the proper license and directs the state LCB to adopt procedures for the issuance of such licenses. On October 16, 2013,[73] the LCB adopted detailed rules for implementing Initiative 502. These rules describe the marijuana license qualifications and application process, application fees, marijuana packaging and labeling restrictions, recordkeeping and security requirements for marijuana facilities, and reasonable time, place, and manner advertising restrictions.[74]

According to the adopted rules, Washington will impose an excise tax of 25% of the selling price on each marijuana sale within the established distribution system.[75] The state excise tax will, therefore, be imposed on three separate transactions: the sale of marijuana from producer to processor, from processor to retailer, and from retailer to consumer. All collected taxes are deposited into the Dedicated Marijuana Fund and distributed, mostly to social and health services, as outlined in the Initiative.[76]

The Initiative also specifically provides that operation of a motor vehicle while under the influence of marijuana remains a crime.[77]

As of the date of this report, recreational marijuana retail stores have yet to open in Washington under the Initiative,[78] although the LCB has received well over 3,000 applications to grow, process, or sell marijuana.[79] The LCB estimated that the application review process may take approximately 90 days to complete and that the state might begin issuing licenses by the end of February 2014.[80]

Colorado

Unlike the relatively specific Washington Initiative 502, Colorado Amendment 64 provides only a general framework for the legalization, regulation, and taxation of marijuana in Colorado— leaving regulatory implementation to the Colorado Department of Revenue.

In November 2012, Colorado voters approved an amendment to the Colorado Constitution to ensure that it "shall not be an offense under Colorado law or the law of any locality within Colorado" for an individual 21 years of age or older to possess, use, display, purchase, consume, or transport one ounce of marijuana; or possess, grow, process, or transport up to six marijuana plants.[81] Unlike Initiative 502, which permits only state-licensed facilities to grow marijuana, Amendment 64 allows any individual over the age of 21 to grow small amounts of marijuana (up to six plants) for personal use.[82] Marijuana may not, however, be consumed "openly and publicly or in a manner that endangers others."[83]

In addition, the amendment also provides that it shall not be unlawful for a marijuana-related facility to purchase, manufacture, cultivate, process, transport, or sell larger quantities of marijuana so long as the facility obtains a current and valid state-issued license.[84] However, the amendment expressly permits local governments within Colorado to regulate or prohibit the operation of such facilities.[85] By comparison, Washington's Initiative 502 does not expressly allow Washington cities to ban marijuana stores from opening within their borders, and there is uncertainty about the degree to which such local prohibitions or moratoriums on the operation of recreational marijuana businesses may be enforced.[86]

Amendment 64 appears to envision a three-tier distribution and regulatory system, similar to that established in Washington, involving the licensing of marijuana cultivation facilities, marijuana product manufacturing facilities, and retail marijuana stores.[87] In December 2012, Governor John Hickenlooper established the Amendment 64 Implementation Task Force (Task Force) to "identify the legal, policy and procedural issues that need to be resolved, and to offer suggestions and proposals ... that need to be taken" to effectively implement Amendment 64.[88] The Task Force issued a final report on March 13, 2013, consisting of 58 recommendations. Of those recommendations, the most significant include establishing a "vertical integration" model in which "cultivation, processing and manufacturing, and retail sales must be a common enterprise under common ownership";[89] imposing the required 15% excise tax while preserving the option for a future marijuana sales tax;[90] restricting commercial licenses to grow, process, or sell marijuana to state residents only;[91] and permitting both residents and nonresidents to purchase marijuana, but imposing more restrictive limits on the quantity of marijuana that may be purchased by out-of-state consumers (a quarter ounce versus an ounce for individuals with a Colorado state-issued identification card).[92]

To implement Amendment 64, the Colorado General Assembly passed three bills that were signed into law by Governor Hickenlooper on May 28, 2013.[93] On September 9, 2013, the Colorado Department of Revenue and State Licensing Authority adopted regulations to implement licensing qualifications and procedures for retail marijuana facilities.[94] The regulations establish procedures for the issuance, renewal, suspension, and revocation of licenses; provide a schedule of licensing and renewal fees; and specify requirements for licensees to follow regarding physical security, video surveillance, labeling, health and safety precautions, and product advertising.[95]

On November 5, 2013, Colorado voters approved a 25% tax on retail marijuana transactions (a 15% excise tax that would raise revenues to be used for public school capital construction, and an additional 10% sales tax that would generate revenues to fund the enforcement of the retail marijuana regulations).[96] On December 23, 2013, the Colorado Marijuana Enforcement Division issued its first recreational marijuana licenses to 348 businesses (136 retail stores, 31 product companies, 178 growing facilities, and 3 testing laboratories).[97] While these businesses have been granted state approval to produce and sell marijuana, they may also have to gain the licensing approval from local governments prior to their operation.[98] On January 1, 2014, 40 licensed retail marijuana stores opened their doors to sell marijuana to anyone 21 years of age or over.[99]

Justice Department Memoranda

The Department of Justice is not required, and realistically lacks the resources, to prosecute every single violation of the CSA. Indeed, pursuant to the doctrine of "prosecutorial discretion," federal law enforcement officials have "broad discretion" as to when, whom, and whether to prosecute for violations of the CSA.[100] Courts have recognized that the "decision to prosecute is particularly ill-suited to judicial review," as it involves the consideration of factors, such as the strength of evidence, deterrence value, and existing enforcement priorities, "not readily susceptible to the kind of analysis the courts are competent to undertake."[101]

Through the exercise of prosecutorial discretion, DOJ is able to develop a policy outlining what marijuana-related activities will receive the most attention from federal authorities. Indeed, DOJ has issued four memoranda since 2009 that explain the Obama Administration's position regarding state-authorized marijuana activities, as described in the following sections.

The 2009 Ogden Memorandum

In 2009, Deputy Attorney General David W. Ogden provided guidance to federal prosecutors in states that have authorized the use of medical marijuana.[102] Citing a desire to make "efficient and rational use of its limited investigative and prosecutorial resources," the memorandum stated that while the "prosecution of significant traffickers of illegal drugs, including marijuana ... continues to be a core priority," federal prosecutors "should not focus federal resources [] on individuals whose actions are in clear and unambiguous compliance with existing state laws providing for the medical use of marijuana."[103] The memorandum made clear, however, that "this guidance [does not] preclude investigation or prosecution, even where there is clear and unambiguous compliance with existing state law, in particular circumstances where investigation or prosecution otherwise serves important federal interests."[104] Nevertheless, the Ogden Memorandum was widely considered an assurance that DOJ would not prosecute any marijuana cultivation, distribution, or possession, as long as those activities complied with state law.[105]

At about the same time, it became apparent the state medical marijuana programs had consequences that were perhaps unintended. In some states, the affliction most easily claimed and most difficult to diagnose—chronic pain—accounted for 90% of all physicians' recommendations.[106] It was said that Los Angeles alone had somewhere between 500 and 1000 medical marijuana dispensaries.[107] No one knew how many for sure, but all agreed there were more dispensaries than there were Starbucks coffee shops.[108] Rather than the old and infirm, "[r]emarkably the age distribution of medical marijuana users seem[ed] to mimic that of recreational users in its concentration of young persons."[109] "After Colorado legalized medical marijuana, the state went from the healthiest in the nation to one with thousands of mostly young adults in need of medical treatment."[110]

The 2011 Cole Memorandum

DOJ reiterated and clarified its position in a subsequent memorandum in 2011 drawing a clear distinction between the potential prosecutions of individual patients who require marijuana in the course of medical treatment and "commercial" dispensaries.[111] After noting that several jurisdictions had recently "enacted legislation to authorize multiple large-scale, privately operated industrial marijuana cultivation centers," DOJ stated that

> The Ogden memorandum was never intended to shield such activities from federal enforcement action and prosecution, even where those activities purport to comply with state law. Persons who are in the business of cultivating, selling or distributing marijuana, and those who knowingly facilitate such activities, are in violation of the [CSA] regardless of state law. Consistent with resource constraints and the discretion you may exercise in your district, such persons are subject to federal enforcement action, including potential prosecution.[112]

The surge in enforcement activity proximate to the release of the 2011 Cole Memorandum[113] caught unawares many of those who considered the Ogden Memorandum a green light for marijuana entrepreneurship.[114]

The 2013 Cole Memorandum

The Obama Administration's official response to the Colorado and Washington initiatives was provided on August 29, 2013, when Deputy Attorney General James M. Cole sent a memorandum to all U.S. Attorneys intended to guide the "exercise of investigative and prosecutorial discretion" when it comes to civil and criminal enforcement of the federal Controlled Substances Act within all states, including those that have legalized marijuana for medicinal or recreational use.[115] The memorandum expresses DOJ's position that, although marijuana is a dangerous drug that remains illegal under federal law, the federal government will not pursue legal challenges against jurisdictions that authorize marijuana in some fashion, assuming those state and local governments maintain strict regulatory and enforcement controls on marijuana cultivation, distribution, sale, and possession that limit the risks to "public safety, public health, and other law enforcement interests." This DOJ decision has received both praise[116] and criticism.[117]

The memorandum instructs federal prosecutors to prioritize their "limited investigative and prosecutorial resources to address the most significant [marijuana-related] threats" and identified the following eight activities as those that the federal government wants most to prevent: (1) distributing marijuana to children; (2) revenue from the sale of marijuana going to criminal enterprises, gangs, and cartels; (3) diverting marijuana from states that have legalized its possession to other states that prohibit it; (4) using state-authorized marijuana activity as a pretext for the trafficking of other illegal drugs; (5) using firearms or violent behavior in the cultivation and distribution of marijuana; (6) exacerbating adverse public health and safety consequences due to marijuana use, including driving while under the influence of marijuana; (7) growing marijuana on the nation's public lands; and (8) possessing or using marijuana on federal property.[118] The memorandum advises U.S. Attorneys and federal law enforcement to devote their resources and efforts toward any individual or organization involved in any of these activities, regardless of state law. Furthermore, the memorandum recommends that jurisdictions that have legalized some form of marijuana activity "provide the necessary resources and demonstrate the willingness to enforce their laws and regulations in a manner that ensures they do not undermine federal enforcement priorities."[119] However, the memorandum cautions that, to the extent that state enforcement efforts fail to sufficiently protect against the eight harms listed above, the federal government retains the right to challenge those states' marijuana laws.

Two additional points made in the memorandum are worth highlighting. First, the memorandum acknowledges a change in Administration policy with respect to "large scale, for-profit commercial enterprises" that may ease the concerns of potential state-licensed marijuana distributors and retailers in Colorado and Washington.[120] In previous guidance issued to U.S. Attorneys in states with medical marijuana laws, DOJ had suggested that large-scale marijuana enterprises were more likely to be involved in marijuana trafficking, and thus could be appropriate targets for federal enforcement actions.[121] In the guidance, DOJ directs prosecutors "not to consider the size or commercial nature of a marijuana operation alone as a proxy for assessing whether marijuana trafficking implicates the Department's enforcement priorities ..."[122]

The memorandum suggests that a state with a robust regulatory system for the control of recreational marijuana "is less likely to threaten [] federal priorities ..." than a state that lacks such controls. This statement may inform the long-running debate over the extent to which state marijuana regulatory and licensing laws (as opposed to mere penalty exemptions) conflict with federal law. Some courts have suggested, for example, that whereas a state is generally free to remove state penalties for marijuana use, the more robust a state's licensing and regulatory program, the more likely the law is to be preempted by federal law.[123] The Oregon Supreme Court, for instance, has suggested that states may not "affirmatively authorize" an individual to participate in conduct prohibited by federal law.[124]

The memorandum makes no statements with regard to the application of various federal money laundering and banking laws that have hampered the ability of commercial marijuana establishments to obtain the necessary financing and financial services to establish and grow their businesses.[125]

The 2014 Cole Memorandum

The 2014 Cole memorandum, however, did address banking and money laundering laws.[126] It recited eight priority points listed in the 2013 memorandum and explained that the same considerations should guide the allocation of investigation and prosecution resources to marijuana-related offenses involving financial transactions—money laundering, money transfers, and Bank Secrecy Act transgressions, discussed later in this report.

PREEMPTION

To what extent does the CSA trump or preempt state medical and recreational marijuana laws? The preemption doctrine stands at the threshold of the federal-state marijuana debate. The preemption doctrine is grounded in the Supremacy Clause of Article VI, cl. 2, which states that "[t]he Constitution, and the Laws of the United States which shall be made in Pursuance thereof; and all Treaties made ... under the Authority of the United States, shall be the supreme Law of the Land."[127] The Supremacy Clause, therefore, "elevates" the U.S. Constitution, federal statutes, federal regulations, and treaties[128] above the laws of the states.[129] As a result, where federal and state law are in conflict, the state law is generally preempted, leaving it void and without effect.[130]

Preemption is a matter of Congress's choice when it operates within its constitutionally enumerated powers. In some instances, Congress has exercised its authority so pervasively as to preclude the possibility of state activity within the same legislative field.[131] On other hand, where Congress prefers the co-existence of state and federal law, state law must give way only when it conflicts with federal law in either of two ways: (1) if it is "physically impossible" to comply with both the state and federal law ("impossibility preemption"); or (2) if the state law "stands as an obstacle to the accomplishment and execution of the full purposes and objectives of Congress" ("obstacle preemption").[132]

What constitutes an obstacle for preemption purposes is a matter "to be informed by examining the federal statute as a whole and identifying its purpose and intended effects."[133] When Congress acts within an area traditionally within the purview of the states, it will be assumed not to have intended to give its words preemptive force unless a contrary purpose is manifestly clear.[134]

The Controlled Substances Act contains an explicit statement of the extent of Congress's preemptive intent. Section 903 provides that

> No provision of this subchapter shall be construed as indicating an intent on the part of the Congress to occupy the field in which that provision operates, including criminal penalties, to the exclusion of any State law on the same subject matter which would otherwise be within the authority of the State, unless there is a positive conflict between that provision of this subchapter and that State law so that the two cannot consistently stand together.[135]

Several state courts have addressed the preemption challenges to state medical marijuana laws with mixed results. Appellate courts in Colorado, California, and Michigan have concluded that at least some aspects of the medical marijuana laws in those states survive both impossibility and obstacle preemption analysis. In two instances, they have held that the language in Section 903 evidences an intent to preempt state laws only under impossibility preemption and *not* under obstacle preemption.[136]

The Colorado case, *People v. Crouse*, arose when a defendant, acquitted of cultivation charges on the basis of immunity under the state medical marijuana law, petitioned the trial court to order police to return of the marijuana plants they had seized in connection with his prosecution.[137] The state questioned whether the CSA precluded such as action. The Court of

Appeals of Colorado determined that a state marijuana law is only in "positive conflict" with the CSA when it is "physically impossible" to simultaneously comply with the state and federal law. It held that in order to preempt the CSA Section 903 "demands more than that the state law 'stands as an obstacle to the accomplishment and execution' of the federal law.'"[138] Thus, the language of the CSA "cannot be used to preempt a state law under the obstacle preemption doctrine."[139] The decision in *Crouse* adopted[140] the reasoning of *County of San Diego v. San Diego NORML*, a California state court decision that also determined that obstacle preemption should not be applied in determining whether a state marijuana law is preempted by the CSA.[141]

In both instances, however, the court supplied an alternative, obstacle preemption explanation. In *Crouse*, the court noted Section 885(d) of the CSA "carves out a specific exemption for distribution of controlled substances by law enforcement officers."[142] Thus, if the officers returned ("distributed") the marijuana to Crouse they would not be not obstructing the CSA but acting in a manner which it authorized.[143]

In *San Diego NORML*, the California law required local governments to issue medical marijuana cards to qualified applicants.[144] In the eyes of the California appellate court, the medical marijuana statute posed no obstacle to the CSA, because "[t]he purpose of the CSA is to combat recreational drug use, not to regulate a state's medical practices."[145]

The Michigan case, *Beek v. City of Wyoming*, involved a Wyoming City property owner and medical marijuana registrant who sought a declarative judgment against a city ordinance which proscribed the use of his property in a manner contrary to federal law including the CSA.[146] Beek argued that the Michigan Medical Marihuana Act (MMMA), which immunized an individual's cultivation of marijuana for medical purposes, invalidated the city ordinance. The City argued that the CSA preempted the MMMA. The Michigan Supreme Court held that the CSA did not preempt the MMMA, but also that ordinance must yield to the MMMA.[147] As understood by the court, the MMMA escaped impossibility preemption because it was permissive and therefore did not command the performance of an act prohibited by federal law: "impossibility results when state law requires what federal law forbids, or vice versa."[148] The MMMA escaped obstacle preemption because it merely conveyed immunity from the consequences of state law: "the MMMA's limited state-law immunity for [medical marijuana] use does not frustrate the CSA's operation nor refuse its provisions their nature effect, such that its purpose cannot otherwise be accomplished.... [T]his immunity does not purport to alter the CSA's federal criminalization of marijuana, or to interfere with or undermine federal enforcement of that prohibition."[149]

The Oregon Supreme Court understood obstacle preemption a little differently in *Emerald Steel.*[150] State regulators had charged Emerald Steel with disability discrimination for firing an employee for medical marijuana use. The Oregon court concluded, based on its interpretation of U.S. Supreme Court precedent, that "[a]ffirmatively authorizing a use that federal law prohibits stands as an obstacle to the implementation and execution of the full purposes and objectives of the Controlled Substances Act."[151] Thus, "[t]o the extent that [the Oregon statute] affirmatively authorizes the use of medical marijuana, federal law preempts that subsection leaving it without effect."[152]

The continued viability of *Emerald Steel* may be open to question. While the Oregon Supreme Court has not overturned its earlier decision, it has observed in *Willis* that *Emerald Steel*'s "affirmative authorization" obstacle preemption test may have been an overgeneralization: "*Emerald Steel* should not be construed as announcing a stand-alone rule that any state law that can be viewed as 'affirmatively authorizing' what federal law prohibits is preempted. Rather it reflects this court's attempt to apply the federal rule and the logic of the most relevant federal cases to the particular preemption problem that was before it. And particularly where, as here, the issue of whether the statute contains an affirmative authorization is not straightforward, the analysis in *Emerald Steel* cannot operate as a simple stand-in for the more general federal rule."[153]

Finally, in what is one of the few reported statements by a federal court relating to preemption of state marijuana laws, in *In re: Rent-Rite Super Kegs West LTD*,[154] a bankruptcy court noted (in what was clearly dicta) that "conflict preemption is not an issue here. Colorado constitutional amendments for both medical marijuana, and the more recent amendment legalizing marijuana possession and usage generally, both make it clear that their provisions apply to state law only. Absent from either enactment is any effort to impede the enforcement of federal law."[155]

OTHER CONSTITUTIONAL CONSIDERATIONS

Other colorable constitutional issues involving the CSA and state medical or recreational marijuana statutes have arisen on a number of occasions. The Supreme Court resolved one of them when it found that Congress's constitutional authority to regulate interstate and foreign commerce enabled it to craft the CSA so as to categorically outlaw the cultivation and possession of marijuana.[156]

Congress's Commerce Clause authority, however, does not include the power to compel a state legislature to act at its bidding or a state official to enforce its will.[157] From time to time, medical marijuana litigants have invoked this limitation in an effort to shield themselves from the CSA. Because the CSA makes no demands of state legislatures or officials, those efforts have been to no avail.[158] The related Tenth Amendment argument that the CSA intrudes upon those police powers reserved to the states has enjoyed no greater success.[159] Of course, the purported exercise of an explicit constitutional power such as the Commerce Clause will be defeated, if the exercise is beyond the scope of the asserted power or is contrary to some other explicit or implicit constitutional limitation.

In the case of the fundamental rights of the people, the Tenth Amendment, the Ninth Amendment, and the substantive due process components of the Fifth and Fourteenth Amendments all impose limits on the federal or state legislative powers.[160] Here too, litigants have been generally unable to convince the courts that the limitations entitle them to relief. Tenth Amendment reservations with respect to the rights of the people disappear once it is established that the Constitution has expressly delegated a power to United States, as in the case of the Necessary and Proper Clause and the CSA.[161] A limitation on intrusion upon the rights of the people, however, may flow from the Ninth Amendment and the Due Process Clauses' implicit prohibition on governmental encroachment on a fundamental right.

Fundamental rights are those "deeply rooted in this Nation's history and tradition, and implicit in the concept of ordered liberty, such that neither liberty nor justice would exist if they were sacrificed."[162] The courts have thus far declined to find such a fundamental right in the possession, use, or cultivation of marijuana, even for medicinal purposes.[163]

Due process and equal protection challenges have surfaced both in cases questioning the CSA and those contesting application of the various state marijuana laws. At the federal level, several courts have rejected the suggestion that the government is estopped from enforcing the CSA by virtue of misleading or inconsistent statements in the Ogden Memorandum and elsewhere.[164] Some of these same cases have rejected the contention that placement of marijuana in Schedule I of the CSA is irrational and consequently constitutes a violation of equal protection.[165]

Municipal zoning or land use ordinances set the stage for most of the state marijuana-related due process cases. State laws vary as to whether municipalities may ban or restrict marijuana-related activities within their jurisdictions.[166] Where they may do so, the regulatory scheme must comply with due process requirements.[167]

BANKING

The federal banking laws are designed to shield financial institutions from individuals and entities that deal in controlled substances. In fact, Congress has crafted several of them to enlist financial institutions in the investigation and prosecution of those who violate the CSA. As a consequence, medical marijuana providers have experienced difficulty securing banking services.[168] On February 14, 2014, the Department of Justice and the Treasury Department's Financial Crimes Enforcement Network (FinCEN) issued guidance with respect to marijuana-related financial crimes.[169] FinCEN's guidance specifically addresses the obligations to file suspicious activity reports.

Banks must file suspicious activity reports (SARs) relating to any transaction involving $5,000 or more that they have reason to suspect are derived from illegal activity.[170] Willful failure to do so is punishable by imprisonment for not more than five years (not more than 10 years in cases of a substantial pattern of violations or transaction involving other illegal activity).[171] Breaking up a transaction into two or more transactions to avoid the reporting requirement subjects the offender to the same 5/10 year maximum terms of imprisonment.[172] Banks must also establish and maintain anti-money laundering programs,[173] designed to ensure that bank officers and employees will have sufficient knowledge of the banks' customers and of the business of those customers to identify the circumstances under which filing SARs is appropriate.[174]

Suspicion aside, banks must file currency transaction reports (CTRs) relating to transactions involving $10,000 or more in cash.[175] Willful failure to do so is punishable by imprisonment for not more than five years (not more than 10 years in cases of a substantial pattern of violations or transaction involving other illegal activity).[176] Again, structuring a transaction to avoid the reporting requirement exposes the offender to the same 5/10 year maximum terms of imprisonment.[177]

Banks, their officers, employees, and customers may also face criminal liability under the money laundering statutes for marijuana-related financial transactions. Section 1957 makes it a federal crime to deposit or withdraw

$10,000 or more in proceeds derived from the distribution of marijuana and any other controlled substances.[178] Section 1956 makes it a federal crime to engage in a financial transaction involving such proceeds conducted with an eye to promoting further offenses, for example, by withdrawing marijuana-generated funds in order to pay the salaries of medical marijuana dispensary employees.[179]

Section 1956 violations are punishable by imprisonment for not more than 20 years.[180] Section 1957 violations are punishable by imprisonment for not more than 10 years.[181] Conspiracy to violate either section carries the same maximum penalties,[182] as does aiding and abetting the commission of either offense.[183] Moreover, any real or personal property involved in, or traceable to, a transaction proscribed by either statute is subject to confiscation under either civil or criminal forfeiture.[184]

Federally insured state and federal banks also run the risk of losing insurance coverage, if they engage in illegal or unsafe banking practices.[185]

In its recent guidance, FinCEN addressed banks' SAR reporting requirements. FinCEN began its guidance by emphasizing the point made in the accompanying 2014 Cole Memorandum, that the Justice Department's investigation and prosecution of financial crimes would be focused on activities that conflict with any of several federal priorities:

- preventing the distribution of marijuana to minors;
- preventing revenue from the sale of marijuana from going to criminal enterprises, gangs, and cartels;[186]
- preventing the diversion of marijuana from states where it is legal under state law in some form to other states;[187]
- preventing state-authorized marijuana activity from being used as a cover or pretext for the trafficking of other illegal drugs or other illegal activity;
- preventing violence and the use of firearms in cultivation and distribution of marijuana;[188]
- preventing drugged driving and the exacerbation of other adverse public health consequences associated with marijuana use;
- preventing the growing of marijuana on public lands and attendant public safety and environmental dangers posed by marijuana production on public lands;[189] and
- preventing marijuana possession or use on federal property.[190]

FinCEN advised financial institutions that in providing services to a marijuana-related business they must file one of three forms of special SARs: a marijuana limited SAR, a marijuana priority SAR; or a marijuana termination SAR. The marijuana limited SAR is appropriate when the bank determines, after the exercise of due diligence, that its customer is not engaged in any of the activities that violate state law or that would implicate any of the Justice Department investigation and prosecution priorities listed in the 2014 Cole Memorandum.[191] A marijuana priority SAR must be filed when the bank believes its customer is engaged in such activities.[192] A bank files a marijuana termination SAR when it finds it necessary to sever its relationship with a customer in order to maintain an effective anti-money laundering program.[193]

FinCEN also provides examples of "red flags" that may indicate that a marijuana priority SAR is appropriate:

- The business is unable to produce satisfactory documentation or evidence to demonstrate that it is duly licensed and operating consistently with state law.
- The business is unable to demonstrate the legitimate source of significant outside investments.
- A customer seeks to conceal or disguise involvement in marijuana-related business activity. For example, the customer may be using a business with a nondescript name (e.g., a "consulting," "holding," or "management" company) that purports to engage in commercial activity unrelated to marijuana, but is depositing cash that smells like marijuana.
- Review of publicly available sources and databases about the business, its owner(s), manager(s), or other related parties, reveal negative information, such as a criminal record, involvement in the illegal purchase or sale of drugs, violence, or other potential connections to illicit activity.
- The business, its owner(s), manager(s), or other related parties are, or have been, subject to an enforcement action by the state or local authorities responsible for administering or enforcing marijuana-related laws or regulations.
- A marijuana-related business engages in international or interstate activity, including by receiving cash deposits from locations outside the state in which the business operates, making or receiving frequent or large interstate transfers, or otherwise transacting with persons or entities located in different states or countries.

- The owner(s) or manager(s) of a marijuana-related business reside outside the state in which the business is located.
- A marijuana-related business is located on federal property or the marijuana sold by the business was grown on federal property.
- A marijuana-related business's proximity to a school is not compliant with state law.
- A marijuana-related business purporting to be a "non-profit" is engaged in commercial activity inconsistent with that classification, or is making excessive payments to its manager(s) or employee(s).
- A customer appears to be using a state-licensed marijuana-related business as a front or pretext to launder money derived from other criminal activity (i.e., not related to marijuana) or derived from marijuana-related activity not permitted under state law. Relevant indicia could include the following:
    - The business receives substantially more revenue than may reasonably be expected given the relevant limitations imposed by the state in which it operates.
    - The business receives substantially more revenue than its local competitors or than might be expected given the population demographics.
    - The business is depositing more cash than is commensurate with the amount of marijuana-related revenue it is reporting for federal and state tax purposes.
    - The business is unable to demonstrate that its revenue is derived exclusively from the sale of marijuana in compliance with state law, as opposed to revenue derived from (i) the sale of other illicit drugs, (ii) the sale of marijuana not in compliance with state law, or (iii) other illegal activity.
    - The business makes cash deposits or withdrawals over a short period of time that are excessive relative to local competitors or the expected activity of the business.
    - Deposits apparently structured to avoid Currency Transaction Report ("CTR") requirements.
    - Rapid movement of funds, such as cash deposits followed by immediate cash withdrawals.
    - Deposits by third parties with no apparent connection to the account holder.

- o Excessive commingling of funds with the personal account of the business's owner(s) or manager(s), or with accounts of seemingly unrelated businesses.
- o Individuals conducting transactions for the business appear to be acting on behalf of other, undisclosed parties of interest.
- o Financial statements provided by the business to the financial institution are inconsistent with actual account activity.
- o A surge in activity by third parties offering goods or services to marijuana-related businesses, such as equipment suppliers or shipping servicers."[194]

The FinCEN guidance ends with the observation that a bank is not absolved of its obligation to file a currency transaction report for any financial transaction involving more than $10,000 in cash, regardless of how it resolves its marijuana SAR obligations.[195]

OTHER FEDERAL LAW CONSEQUENCES

Employment

The use of marijuana, medicinal or otherwise, may have adverse employment consequences.[196] Both state and federal courts have upheld firing an employee for medical marijuana use.[197] Employee challenges have cited in vain state medical marijuana laws as well as federal and state anti-discrimination laws. The state medical marijuana laws ordinarily immunize medical marijuana users from the adverse consequences of the law, but do not give them a right that can be used affirmatively against a private entity.[198] The Americans with Disabilities Act (ADA) and similar state anti-discrimination in employment statutes are predicated upon discrimination based on *lawful* activity and the CSA has consequently proven to be an insurmountable obstacle.[199]

They differ somewhat in the case of nongovernment employees, because, among other things, federal, state, and local government employees enjoy Fourth Amendment protections. The Fourth Amendment, binding on government employers, does not give employees the right to use marijuana, medical or otherwise, but it limits the likelihood that their employers will discover their use. The Fourth Amendment's proscription on unreasonable governmental searches means that federal, state, or local entities must have either reasonable suspicion or a constitutionally recognized special need in order to conduct employee drug testing.[200]

Government

A significant number of government employees, however, must undergo random drug testing because the nature of their duties places them in a "special needs" category. For example, random drug testing is a fact of life and continued condition of employment for anyone with access to classified or similarly sensitive information.[201]

In the case of employees of state or local governmental entities, the "lower courts have allowed drug testing in other safety-sensitive occupation" such as "aviation personnel, railroad safety inspectors, highway and motor carrier safety specialists, lock and dam operators, forklift operators, tractor operators, engineering operators, and crane operators."[202]

More generally, federal contractors may face the loss of federal funding or could be subject to administrative fines if they do not maintain and enforce policies aimed at achieving a drug-free, safe workplace. The federal Drug-Free Workplace Act of 1988 (DFWA)[203] imposes a drug-free workplace requirement on any entity that receives federal contracts with a value of more than $150,000 or that receives any federal grant.[204] DFWA requires these entities to make ongoing, good faith efforts to comply with the drug-free workplace requirement in order to qualify, and remain eligible, for federal funds.[205]

Private

Absent status as a federal contractor and grantee status or some other federal influence,[206] employers are relatively free to establish their own drug free workplaces and to fire employees who test positive for marijuana use, medical or otherwise.[207] Although an occasional medical marijuana statute will shield employees,[208] more often the statute is silent and thought not to cabin at will employment status, as noted earlier.[209] Moreover, depending upon the factual situation and the state unemployment statute in play, employees fired for marijuana use may also be ineligible for unemployment benefits.[210]

Taxation

Income from any source is ordinarily subject to federal taxation.211 This is so even when the activity that generates the income is unlawful.212

Marijuana merchants, however, operate under a special federal tax disadvantage. They cannot deduct their operating expenses. Most businesses, similarly situated, arrive at their taxable income after deducting the cost of things like employee salaries, rent or mortgage payments, legal services, state taxes, and equipment depreciation.213 Marijuana merchants may take no such deductions:

> No deduction or credit shall be allowed for any amount paid or incurred during the taxable year in carrying on any trade or business if such trade or business (or the activities which comprise such trade or business) consists of trafficking in controlled substances (within the meaning of schedule I and II of the Controlled Substances Act) which is prohibited by Federal law or the law of any State in which such trade or business is conducted.[214]

Several Members of Congress asked for Internal Revenue Service (IRS) guidance in order to allow marijuana merchants operating in a medical marijuana state to deduct their business expenses. The IRS responded that they would be unable to do so until Congress amended either the Internal Revenue Code or the CSA.[215] Moreover, the customers of a medical marijuana merchant may be unable to treat their purchases as deductible medical expenses.[216]

Possession of Firearms

It is a federal crime punishable by imprisonment for not more than 10 years for an unlawful user of a controlled substance to possess a firearm or ammunition.[217] Federal regulations define an "unlawful user" to include "any person who is a current user of a controlled substance in a manner other than as prescribed by a licensed physician."[218] The Bureau of Alcohol, Tobacco, Firearms and Explosives (ATF) has made it clear that "any person who uses ... marijuana, regardless of whether his or her State has passed legislation authorizing marijuana use for medicinal purposes, is an unlawful user of ... a controlled substance, and is prohibited by Federal law from possessing firearms or ammunition."[219]

Moreover, those associated with a marijuana-cultivation or -sales operation may incur additional firearm-related criminal liability. In addition to the penalties for growing or selling, anyone who provides security for the operation and possesses a firearm in furtherance of that enterprise is subject to a series of mandatory terms of imprisonment.[220] The offender and any accomplices face an additional five-year mandatory minimum term of imprisonment for possession of a firearm; a seven-year mandatory term if he brandishes the firearm; and a 10-year mandatory term if discharges it.[221]

Federally Assisted Housing

"Illegal drug users" are ineligible for federally assisted housing.[222] Public housing agencies and owners of federally assisted housing must establish standards that would allow the agency or owner to prohibit admission to, or terminate the tenancy or assistance of, any applicant or tenant who is an illegal drug user.[223] An agency or an owner can take these actions if a determination is made, pursuant to the standards established, that an individual is "illegally using a controlled substance," or if there is reasonable cause to believe that an individual has a "pattern of illegal use" of a controlled substance that could "interfere with the health, safety, or right to a peaceful enjoyment of the premises by other residents."[224] Thus, any individual whom the housing authority reasonably believes is using marijuana could be denied access to, or evicted from, federally assisted housing.

With respect to medical marijuana, the Department of Housing and Urban Development previously concluded that public housing agencies or owners "must deny *admission*" to applicants who are using medical marijuana, but "have statutorily-authorized discretion with respect to evicting or refraining from evicting *current residents* on account of their use of medical marijuana."[225]

The question of whether marijuana users may be excluded from federally assisted housing is not the same as whether applicants for such housing may be required to undergo drug testing. The Eleventh Circuit's *Labron* decision, decided in another context, would seem to preclude such preliminary testing in the absence of some individualized suspicion.[226]

ETHICAL CONSIDERATIONS

Rule 1.2(d) of the American Bar Association's Model Rules of Professional Conduct, adopted in virtually every jurisdiction, states that "A lawyer shall not counsel a client to engage, or assist a client, in conduct that the lawyer knows is criminal or fraudulent, but a lawyer may discuss the legal consequences of any proposed course of conduct with a client and may counsel or assist a client to make a good-faith effort to determine the validity, scope, meaning or application of the law."[227]

Bar officials in several states—Arizona, Colorado, Connecticut, Maine, and Washington, among them—have issued ethics opinions addressing ethical constraints arising out of the conflict between state and federal marijuana laws.[228]

The Arizona State Bar concluded in Opinion 11-01that the Ogden Memorandum had created a "safe harbor" for those that operated within the confines of the state's medical marijuana statute.[229] In its view, Arizona lawyers may counsel and assist their clients in any activity permitted under the Arizona medical marijuana law as long as their clients were made fully aware of the consequences under federal law.[230]

In contrast, Opinion 199 of the Maine Professional Ethics Commission advised attorneys that, absent an amendment to either the Rules of Professional Conduct or the CSA, a member of the Maine bar "may counsel or assist a client in making good faith efforts to determine the validity, scope, meaning or application of the law," but "the Rule forbids attorneys from counseling a client to engage in the [marijuana] business or to assist the a client in doing so."[231] The Commission declined to provide more specific advice, but warned that significant risks attended practice in the area.

The Connecticut Bar Association offered much the same advice.[232] Lawyers may advise their clients about the features of the state medical marijuana statute, but they may not assist clients in a violation of the CSA.

While the Arizona, Maine, and Connecticut opinions are relatively general and relatively terse, the Colorado opinion provides far more examples of its view of the permissible and impermissible.[233] It concluded that, consist with Rule 1.2(d) and the CSA, a Colorado attorney might (1) represent and advise a client concerning the consequences of marijuana-related activities for purposes of criminal law, family law, or labor law; (2) as a government attorney advise a client in a matter involving the establishing, interpreting, enforcing, or amending zoning relations, local ordinances, or legislation;[234] or (3) advise a client on the tax obligations incurred when cultivating or selling marijuana.

It concluded, on the other hand, that a Colorado attorney may not (1) draft or negotiate contracts, leases, or other agreements to facilitate the cultivate, distribution, or consumption of marijuana; or (2) provide tax planning assistance with an eye to violating federal law. Moreover, the Opinion points out that providing such assistance while aware of a client's intent is "likely to constitute aiding and abetting the violation of or conspiracy to violate federal law."

The Opinion contains an addendum that indicates that the Colorado Supreme Court has been asked to amend the Rules of Professional Conduct to remove the shadow of the CSA from the application of the Rules to legal services provided within the confines of the state marijuana laws.[235]

Washington State attorneys have the advantage of not one, but two bar advisories. Both take a position similar to the Arizona opinion: attorneys transgress no ethical boundaries if their professional conduct is consistent with state law and perhaps with federal enforcement priorities. The Bar Association of King County (Seattle and environs) opined that an attorney who advises and assists a client to establish and maintain a marijuana dispensary is not subject to discipline, as long as his client's conduct is permitted under state marijuana law and as long as he makes his client aware of the provisions of the CSA including the Cole Memorandum.[236]

Moreover, in the opinion of the King County Bar Association, an attorney is likewise not subject to discipline merely because he owns an interest in a marijuana dispensary. Although such activity may constitute a crime under the CSA, it is not "a criminal act that reflects adversely on the lawyer's honesty, trustworthiness or fitness as a lawyer," in the eyes of the County Bar Association.

The second Washington opinion is a proposed advisory opinion which the Washington State Bar Association submitted to the Washington Supreme Court along with a proposal to add a comment to Rule 1.2 of the Washington Rules of Professional Conduct.[237] In its proposed opinion, a lawyer would be free to advise a client as to the nuances of state marijuana law as long as he did not do so in furtherance of an effort to violate or mask a violation of state marijuana law. A lawyer would also be free to advise and assist a client to establish and maintain a dispensary within the bounds of state law at least until such time as federal enforcement policies change. Finally, under the proposed opinion and accompanying proposed comment, a lawyer would be free to engage in a marijuana business without offending the Rule that condemns criminal conduct that reflects adversely on a lawyer's fitness to practice.[238]

Marijuana Research under Federal Law

The federal government retains strict controls over the use of marijuana for research purposes. Under the CSA, the Attorney General, as delegated to the Drug Enforcement Agency (DEA), is authorized to register "practitioners" to "dispense, or conduct research with" controlled substances.[239] In instances where the practitioner seeks to conduct research on a schedule I drug, such as marijuana, that application is forwarded to the Secretary of Health and Human Services "who shall determine the qualifications and competency of each practitioner requesting registration, as well as the merits of the research protocol."[240] The Secretary is also directed to "consult" with the Attorney General to ensure "effective procedures to adequately safeguard against diversion of such controlled substances from legitimate medical or scientific use."[241] As of January 2013, the DEA has registered approximately 125 practitioners to conduct marijuana research.[242]

Practitioners obtain marijuana for approved research through the National Institute on Drug Abuse (NIDA) drug supply program. Under the CSA, the Attorney General is authorized to register applicants to manufacture or grow marijuana "if he determines that such registration is consistent with the public interest and with United States obligations under international treaties ..."[243] Currently, the National Center for Natural Products Research (NCNPR) at the University of Mississippi is the only organization registered to manufacture marijuana.[244] The National Institute on Drug Abuse (NIDA) administers the federal contract with the NCNPR and therefore acts as the "single official source" through which researchers may obtain marijuana for research purposes.[245]

CONGRESSIONAL RESPONSE IN THE 113TH CONGRESS

Several proposals concerning marijuana have been introduced that reflect different approaches in response to the state legalization initiatives.

P.L. 113-79 (H.R. 2642), Agricultural Act of 2014. This public law has two marijuana related sections. One relates to food stamps, the other to industrial hemp. Eligibility for the receipt of benefits under the Supplemental Nutrition Assistance Program (SNAP)(food stamps) is governed in part by a means test. Only individuals below a certain income level are eligible. Section 4005 of P.L. 113-79 (7 U.S.C. §2014(e)(5)(C)) instructs the Secretary of Agriculture to promulgate rules to ensure that the costs of medical marijuana are not treated as a deduction in that calculation. Comparable provisions appeared *in H.R. 3102, the Nutrition Reform and Work Opportunity Act of 2013* (Section 106) and *H.R. 1947, the Federal Agriculture Reform and Risk Management Act of 2013* (Section 4006). Section 7606 of P.L. 113-79 authorizes institutions of higher education and state departments of agriculture to grow and cultivate industrial hemp for research purposes.

H.R. 499, Ending Federal Marijuana Prohibition Act of 2013. This bill would direct the Attorney General to issue a final order, within 60 days of the bill's enactment, that entirely removes marijuana from any CSA schedule.[246] In addition, the bill would amend the CSA by adding a new Section 103 that declares that no provision of the CSA shall apply to marijuana, with the following new exception: shipping or transporting marijuana from anywhere outside a jurisdiction of the United States into such a jurisdiction where marijuana use, possession, or sale is prohibited.[247] The bill would make conforming amendments to the CSA as well as other sections of the *U.S. Code* to expressly remove the word "marijuana" or "marihuana" from various penalty, enforcement, and definition provisions.[248] The bill also would amend the Federal Alcohol Administration Act[249] to create a new section entitled "Unlawful Businesses Without Marijuana Permit."[250] This section would make it unlawful to engage in importing, shipping, or selling marijuana in interstate or foreign commerce, or cultivating, producing, manufacturing, packaging, or warehousing marijuana, without a permit issued by the Secretary of the Treasury. The criminal fine for persons engaging in such activity without a permit would be not more than $1,000, although the Secretary would be allowed to collect a payment from the violator of up to $500 in lieu of referring the violation to the Attorney General for prosecution. The Secretary would have to follow specific eligibility criteria set forth in the bill in selecting applicants for a marijuana business permit and the Secretary would also be required to establish a reasonable permit fee to cover the cost of implementing and overseeing all aspects of federal regulation of marijuana.

Finally, the bill would grant the Food and Drug Administration the same authorities with respect to marijuana as it has with respect to alcohol,[251] and would transfer all current functions of the DEA Administrator relating to marijuana enforcement to the Director of the Bureau of Alcohol, Tobacco, Firearms and Explosives.[252]

H.R. 501, Marijuana Tax Equity Act of 2013. This bill would amend the Internal Revenue Code to impose an excise tax on the sale of marijuana by the producer or importer of the drug, equivalent to 50% of the price for which it was sold.[253] In addition, the bill would require anyone engaged in a "marijuana enterprise"[254] to pay an occupational tax in the amount of $1,000 per year (for producers, importers, or manufacturers of marijuana), or $500 per year (for distributors, retailers, or anyone who transports, stores, or displays marijuana products).[255] The bill would require all individuals, prior to commencing business as a marijuana enterprise, to obtain a permit from the Secretary of the Treasury.[256] Finally, the bill would impose civil and criminal penalties for violation of the duty to pay the new taxes regarding marijuana as well as engaging in business as a marijuana enterprise without obtaining the requisite permit.[257] The bill does not amend the CSA the provisions of which would thus remain in effect.

H.R. 689, States' Medical Marijuana Patient Protection Act. This bill would direct the Secretary of Health and Human Services, in cooperation with the National Academy of Sciences' Institute of Medicine, to submit to the DEA Administrator a recommendation on the scheduling of marijuana within the CSA, although the bill precludes the Secretary from selecting either Schedule I or II.[258] The Secretary would be required to issue such recommendation within 180 days of the enactment of the bill, and the DEA Administrator would need to issue a proposed rulemaking for the rescheduling of marijuana in accordance with the recommendation within a year of enactment of the bill.[259] The legislation declares that no provision of the CSA, nor any provision of the Federal Food, Drug, and Cosmetic Act,[260] shall prohibit or otherwise restrict in a state where the medical use of marijuana is lawful under state law, the production, prescription, transportation, distribution, possession, or use of marijuana for medical use.[261] Finally, the bill would require the Attorney General, within 180 days of the bill's enactment, to transfer control over access to marijuana for research purposes (currently the responsibility of the National Institute on Drug Abuse, a component of the National Institutes of Health, U.S. Department of Health and Human Services) to an executive branch entity "that is not focused on researching the addictive properties of substances."[262] The bill would require such entity to "take appropriate actions to ensure that an adequate supply of marijuana is available for therapeutic and medicinal research."[263]

H.R. 710, Truth in Trials Act. This bill would amend the federal criminal code (Title 18 of the *U.S. Code*) to provide an affirmative defense for conduct regarding the medical use of marijuana in a prosecution or proceeding for any marijuana-related offense under any federal law. Individuals asserting such defense must establish, by a preponderance of the evidence, that their marijuana-related activities were conducted in compliance with state law regarding medical use of marijuana.[264] The bill would require that any property seized by the government in connection with such prosecution or proceeding be returned to the owner within 10 days of the court finding that the owner has established a valid affirmative defense.[265] Finally, the bill would permit a court to hold liable for the marijuana-related offense a defendant who has engaged primarily, but not exclusively, in medical marijuana activities, only with respect to the amount of marijuana that was used for nonmedical purposes.[266]

H.R. 784, States' Medical Marijuana Property Rights Protection Act. This bill would amend the civil forfeiture provisions of the CSA[267] to provide that no real property may be subject to civil forfeiture to the United States due to medical marijuana-related activities that are performed in compliance with state law.[268]

H.R. 964, Respect States' and Citizens' Rights Act of 2013. This bill would amend the CSA's preemption provision, Section 708 (codified at 21 U.S.C. §903), to provide a specific rule of construction pertaining to state marijuana laws: that no provision of the CSA shall be construed as—(1) indicating an intent on the part of Congress to occupy the field in which that provision operates, including criminal penalties, to the exclusion of state law regarding marijuana, or (2) preempting any such state law.[269] The bill may or may not be intended to preclude enforcement of the CSA's marijuana provisions, regardless the status of marijuana under state law.

H.R. 1523, Respect State Marijuana Laws Act of 2013. This bill would amend federal law to provide that no provision of the CSA related to marijuana may be applied to any person acting in compliance with state laws relating to marijuana.

H.R. 1635, National Commission on Federal Marijuana Policy Act of 2013. This bill would establish a federal commission to undertake a comprehensive review of current federal policies toward marijuana.

H.R. 2652, Marijuana Businesses Access to Banking Act of 2013. This bill would provide legal immunity from federal criminal prosecution to banks and credit unions, their officers and employees that provide financial services to marijuana-related businesses that engage in activities pursuant to state law ("marijuana related legitimate business").[270] It would protect from criminal, civil, or administrative forfeiture a depository institution's interest for a loan related to such a business.[271] It would not otherwise shield financial institutions from any civil or administrative forfeiture that might attend the services it provides to marijuana businesses. The bill would, however, absolve financial institutions of the suspicious activity reports they might otherwise be required to file with respect to the services to provide for marijuana-related legitimate businesses.[272] Finally, it would bar federal bank regulators from jeopardizing a depository bank's federally insured status based on its relationship with marijuana-related legitimate business.[273]

H.R. 3483, Protecting Individual Liberties and States' Rights Act. This bill would amend federal firearms law. Existing law denies users of controlled substances or those with a prior felony conviction the right to purchase or possess firearms or ammunition. The bill would amend these provisions to remove from the felony disqualification a federal conviction related to marijuana in a state where the conduct was lawful and to remove from the marijuana user disqualification instances where the possession is lawful under state law and the user is a resident of the state.

H.R. 4046, Unmuzzle the Drug Czar Act of 2014. This bill would delete from existing law the provision that prohibits the Office of National Drug Control Policy from expending federal funds for any study or contract relating to the legalization of any Schedule I controlled substances such as marijuana.

H.R. 4137, Preserving Welfare for Needs Not Weed Act. This bill would add marijuana dispensaries to the list of business in which Temporary Assistance for Needy Families (TANF) credits may not be used.

H.R. 4142, No Welfare for Weed Act of 2014. This bill would add marijuana dispensaries to the list of businesses in which Temporary Assistance for Needy Families (TANF) credits may not be used. It would also amend the definition of "food" for purposes of the food stamp (SNAP) program to exclude marijuana products.

H.R. 4179, Lucid Act. This bill would amend federal law relating to highway assistance to the states to add driving under the influence of marijuana requirements to the existing drunk driving requirements.

End Notes

[1] Section 202(c) of the Controlled Substances Act (21 U.S.C. §812(c), Sch.I(c)(10)).

[2] The terms "recreational marijuana laws" and "retail marijuana laws" are used interchangeably in this report. Some legislators, advocates, and commentators refer to the laws alternatively as "recreational marijuana laws," "retail marijuana laws," "adult social marijuana laws," or "states' rights marijuana laws." E.g., Malanie, Reid, The Quagmire that Nobody in the Federal Government Wants to Talk About: Marijuana, 44 N.MEX. L.REV. 169, 171 (2014) ("Colorado and Washington have legalized marijuana use for recreational purposes"); Sam Kamin & Eli Wald, Marijuana Lawyers: Outlaws or Crusaders, 91 ORE. L. REV. 869, 878 n.35 (2013)("Many in the marijuana law reform movement dislike the term 'recreational use' and prefer the phrase 'adult use.' ... 'I don't use the term recreational, I prefer adult social use'"); H.R. 964 (Respect States' and Citizens' Rights Act of 2013); Colorado Retail Marijuana Code, COLO. REV. STAT. ANN. §§12-43.4-101 et seq.

[3] 38 Stat. 785 (1914).

[4] U.S. Const. Art. I, §8, cls. 1, 3, 18; Art. II, §2, cl.2.

[5] H.Rept. 63-23, at 1 (1913)("... [T]he obligations by which [the United States] is bound by virtue of the international opium convention signed at the Hague January 23, 1912, should be sufficient evidence of the necessity for the passage of Federal legislation to control our foreign and interstate traffic in opium, coca leaves, their salts, derivatives, and preparations.... But there is a real and, one might say, even desperate need of Federal legislation to control our foreign and interstate traffic in habit-forming drugs, and to aid both directly and indirectly the States more effectually to enforce their police laws designed to restrict narcotics to legitimate medical channels"), quoted in accord, S.Rept. 63- 258, at 3 (1914).

[6] 50 Stat. 551 (1937).

[7] H.Rept. 75-792. at 1-3. (1937)("The purpose of H.R. 6906 is to employ the Federal taxing power to raise revenue from the marihuana drug traffic and to discourage the widespread use of the drug by smokers and drug addicts.... This bill is modeled upon both the Harrison Narcotics Act and the National Firearms Act, which were designed to accomplish these same general objectives with respect to opium and coca leaves, and firearms, respectively.... Your committee has examined the constitutionality of this bill and is satisfied that it is a valid revenue measure. The law is well settled that a revenue measure will not be held invalid as an attempt to regulate, under the guise of the taxing power, a subject matter reserved to the States under the tenth amendment, if it appears on its face to be a revenue measure and contains no regulatory provisions except those reasonably related to the collection of the revenue.... In addition, certain provisions of the bill may be sustained under the power of Congress to regulate commerce and the power of Congress over the District of Columbia and Territories and possessions of the United States"); see also, S.Rept. 75-900, at 2-3 (1937)("The purpose of H.R. 6906 is to employ the Federal taxing power to raise revenue from the marihuana drug traffic and to discourage the widespread use of the drug by smokers an drug addicts.... This bill is modeled upon both the Harrison Narcotics Act and the National Firearms Act, which were designed to accomplish these same general objectives with respect to opium and coca leaves, and firearms, respectively")(but including no other explicit reference to constitutional authority).

[8] Marihuana Tax Act, §§2-14, 50 Stat. 551-56 (1937).

[9] Id. at §7(e), 50 Stat. 555 (1937)("All provisions of law (including penalties) applicable in respect of the taxes imposed by the Act of December 17, 1914 (38 Stat. 785; U.S.C. 1934 ed. title 26, §§1040-1061, 1383-1391), as amended, shall, insofar as not inconsistent with this Act, be applicable in respect of the taxes imposed by this Act").

[10] The President's Commission on Law Enforcement and Administration of Justice: Task Force on Narcotics and Drug Abuse, Task Force Report: Narcotics and Drug Abuse, 12 (1967).

[11] Marchetti v. United States, 390 U.S. 39, 48 (1968); see also, Grosso v. United States, 390 U.S. 62, 64-6 (1968).

[12] Haynes v. United States, 390 U.S. 85, 100 (1968).

[13] Leahy v. United States, 395 U.S. 6, 29 (1969).

[14] S.Rept. 91-613 (1969). In Gonzales v. Raich, the U.S. Supreme Court ruled that Congress had the constitutional authority under the Commerce Clause to prohibit the wholly intrastate cultivation or possession of marijuana for medical purposes, despite state laws that permit such activity. 545 U.S. 1, 32-3 (2005); for more information about this decision, see CRS Report RL32844, The Power to Regulate Commerce: Limits on Congressional Power, by Kenneth R. Thomas.

[15] S.Rept. 91-613 at 1-2.

[16] Id. at 10 ("The study shall include, but need not be limited to, the following matters: 1. Identification of existing gaps in our knowledge of marihuana. 2. An intensive examination of the important medical and social aspects of marihuana use. 3. Surveys of the extent and nature of marijuana use. 4. Studies of the pharmacology and effects of marihuana. 5. Studies of the relation of marihuana use to crime and juvenile delinquency. 6. Studies of the relation between marihuana and the use of other drugs").

[17] National Commission on Marihuana and Drug Abuse, Drug Use in America: Problem in Prospective, 458, 466 (2d Rep. 1973).

[18] 21 U.S.C. §§801 et seq.

[19] P.L. 91-513, 84 Stat. 1236 (1970).

[20] 21 U.S.C. §§811-812.

[21] The Attorney General delegated his authority under the CSA to the DEA Administrator pursuant to 21 U.S.C. §871(a); 28 C.F.R. §0.100(b).

[22] For more information about these requirements, see CRS Report RL34635, The Controlled Substances Act: Regulatory Requirements, by Brian T. Yeh.

[23] 21 U.S.C. §812(b)(1).

[24] 21 U.S.C. §823(f).

[25] See 21 C.F.R. §1306.03 (persons entitled to issue prescriptions).

[26] 21 C.F.R. §1306.04; United States v. Moore, 4223 U.S. 122 (1975).

[27] The procedures for these actions are found at 21 U.S.C. §811.

[28] 21 U.S.C. §811(a).

[29] At one point an administrative law judge did recommend rescheduling, but that represents the high water mark for the petition efforts; see, generally, Americans for Safe Access v. DEA, 706 F.3d 438 (D.C. Cir. 2013); and Alliance for Cannabis Therapeutics v. DEA, 15 F.3d 1131, 1133 (D.C. 1994), citing, National Organization for the Reform of Marijuana Laws v. Ingersoll, 497 F.2d 654 (D.C. Cir. 1974); National Organization for the Reform of Marijuana Laws v. Drug Enforcement Administration, 559 F.2d 735 (D.C. Cir. 1977); National Organization for the Reform of Marijuana Laws v. Department of Health, Education and Welfare, No. 79-1660 (D.C. Cir. Oct. 16, 1980); Alliance for Cannabis Therapeutics v. DEA, 930 F.2d 936 (D.C. Cir. 1991).

[30] For a detailed description of the CSA's civil and criminal provisions, see CRS Report RL30722, Drug Offenses: Maximum Fines and Terms of Imprisonment for Violation of the Federal Controlled Substances Act and Related Laws, by Brian T. Yeh.

[31] 21 U.S.C. §812(c).

[32] Very narrow exceptions to the federal prohibition do exist. For example, one may legally use marijuana if participating in an FDA-approved study or participate in the Compassionate Investigational New Drug program.

[33] 21 U.S.C. §844(a).

[34] 21 U.S.C. §844(a).

[35] The escalating terms of imprisonment for possession of various amounts of marijuana are as follows: (1) Less than 50 kilograms (110lbs.)/fewer than 50 plants: imprisonment for not more than 5 years, 21 U.S.C. §841(b)(1)(D); (2) Less than 100 kilograms (220lbs) or less than 100 plants: imprisonment for not more than 20 years, 21 U.S.C. §841(b)(1)(C); (3) 100 kilograms (220lbs) or more /100 plants or more: imprisonment for not less than 5 years or more 40 years, 21 U.S.C. §841(b)(1)(B); (4) 1000 kilograms or more/1000 plants or more: imprisonment for not less than 10 years or more than life, 21 U.S.C. §841(b)(1)(A); (5) Drug kingpin (over 5 or more others & substantial income): imprisonment for not less than 20 years or more than life, 21 U.S.C. §848(a), (c); and (6) Drug kingpin involving (a)

30,000 kilograms or more/30,000 plants or more, or (b) $10 million or more in annual gross receipts: imprisonment for life, 21 U.S.C. §848(b)(2).

[36] 21 U.S.C. §853 (criminal forfeiture of the proceeds and property derived from a violation as well as property used to facilitate violation); 21 U.S.C. §881 (civil/administrative forfeiture of conveyances and real property used in a violation and the proceeds of a violation and property traceable to the proceeds of a violation).

[37] U.S. CONST. amend. V ("No person shall ... be deprived of ... property, without due process of law ...").

[38] Calero-Toledo v. Pearson Yacht Leasing Co, 416 U.S. 663, 683-90 (1974)(confiscation of a yacht upon which those to whom it was leased smoke marijuana, because the owners failed to show that they had done all they possibly could to avoid the illegal use of their property). In controlled substances cases, there is a limited statutory innocent owner defense if the owner of an interest in the property can show by a preponderance of the evidence that either he "(i) did not know of the conduct giving rise to the forfeiture; or (ii) upon learning of the conduct giving rise to the forfeiture, did all that reasonably could be expected under the circumstances to terminate such use of the property," 18 U.S.C. §983(d).

[39] For a more extensive discussion of forfeiture generally, see CRS Report 97-139, Crime and Forfeiture, by Charles Doyle.

[40] See, e.g., 21 U.S.C. §881(a)(6) (proceeds), and 21 U.S.C. §881(a)(2) (products and equipment used to facilitate the offense).

[41] 21 U.S.C. §881(a) (emphasis added).

[42] 18 U.S.C. §981(b).

[43] 21 U.S.C. §881(e).

[44] 21 U.S.C. §881(e).

[45] See, e.g., U.S. Dep't of Justice, Press Release: Federal Authorities Take Enforcement Actions Against Commercial Marijuana Stores in Orange County Cities of Anaheim and La Habra, August 21, 2012, available at http://www.justice.gov/usao/cac/Pressroom/2012/111.html.

[46] See David Downs, City of Oakland Loses Lawsuit Against Department of Justice; Harborside Forfeiture Case Proceeds, February 15, 2013, EAST BAY EXPRESS, available at http://www.eastbayexpress.com/LegalizationNation/ archives/2013/02/15/city-of-oakland-loses-lawsuit-against-department-of-justice-harborside-forfeiture-case-proceeds (describing how a federal magistrate judge dismissed the City of Oakland's lawsuit against Attorney General Eric Holder and U.S. Attorney Melinda Haag, which sought to prevent Haag from seizing the building leased by Harborside Health Center, one of the world's largest medical marijuana dispensaries. The judge held that only the dispensary and its landlords have legal standing to challenge the U.S. government's attempted seizure of the property.).

[47] ALA. CODE §§20-2-1 to 20-2-190; ALASKA STAT. §§11.71.010 to 11.71.900, 17.30.010 to 17.30.900; ARIZ. REV. STAT. ANN. §§36-2501 to 36-2553; ARK. CODE ANN. §§5-64-101 to 5-64-608; CAL. HEALTH & SAFETY CODE §§11000 to 11657; COLO. REV. STAT. ANN. §§18-18-101 to 18-18-605; CONN. GEN. STAT. ANN. §§21a-240 to 21a-283; Del. Code Ann. tit.16 §§4701 to 47696; FLA. STAT. ANN. §§893.01 to 893.165; GA. CODE §§16-13-20 to 16-13-65; HAWAII REV. STAT. §§329-1 to 329-128; IDAHO CODE §§37-2701 to 37-2751; 720 ILL. COMP. STAT. ANN. §§570/100 to 570/603; IND. CODE ANN. §§35-48-1-1 to 35-48-7-15; IOWA CODE ANN. §§124.101 to 124.602; KAN. STAT. ANN. §§65 41-1 to 65-4166; KY. REV. STAT. ANN. §§218A.010 to 218A.993; LA. REV. STAT. ANN. §§40:961 to 40:995; ME. REV. STAT. ANN. tit.17-A §§1101 to 1118; MD. CODE ANN. Crim. Law §§5-101 to 5-1101; MASS. GEN. LAWS ANN. ch. 94C §§1 to 48; Mich. Comp. Laws Ann. §§333.7101 to 333.7545; MINN. STAT.

ANN. §§152.01 to 152.20; MISS. CODE ANN. §§41-29-101 to 41-29-185; MO. ANN. STAT. §§195.010 to 195.320; MONT. CODE ANN. §§50-32-101 to 50-32-405; NEB. REV. STAT. §§28-401 to 28-457; NEV. REV. STAT. §§453.011 to 453.740; N.H. REV. STAT. ANN. §§318-B:1 to 318-E:1; N.J. STAT. ANN. §§2C:35-1 to 2C:35-24, 2c:36-1 to 2C:36-10, 24:21-1 to 24-21-54; N.MEX. STAT. ANN. §§30 31-1 to 30-31-41; N.Y. PUBLIC HEALTH LAW §§3300 to 3396; N.C. GEN. STAT. §§90-86 to 90-113.8; N.D. CENT. CODE §§19-03.1-01to 19-03.1-46; OHIO REV. CODE ANN. §§3719.01 to 3719.99; OKLA. STAT. ANN. tit.63 §§2-101 to 2-610; ORE. REV. STAT. §§475.005 to 475.295, 475.940 to 475.999; 35 PA. STAT. ANN. §§780-101 to780-144; R.I. GEN. LAWS §§21-28-1.01 to 21-28-6.02; S.C. CODE ANN. §§44-53-110 to 44-53-590; S.D. COD. LAWS §§34-20B-1 to 34-20B-114; TENN. CODE ANN. §§39-17-401 to 39-17-434, 53-11-301 to 53-11-452; TEX. HEALTH & SAFETY CODE ANN. §§481.001 to 481.005; UTAH CODE ANN. §§58-37-1 to 58-37-21; VA. CODE §§54.1-3400 to 54.1-3472; WASH. REV. CODE ANN. §§69.50.101 to 69.50.609; W.VA. CODE ANN. §§60A-1-101 to 60A-6-605; WIS. STAT. ANN. §§961.001 to 961.62; WYO. STAT. §§35-7-1001 to 35-7-1062. Vermont has a Regulated Drugs Act that roughly corresponds to the Controlled Substances Act, VT. STAT. ANN. tit.18 §§4201 to 4254.

[48] E.g., ALASKA STAT. §§11.71.190, 11.71.060, 12.55.135(j) (max. fine $500/less than 1 oz.); CAL. HEALTH & SAFETY CODE §11357(b) (max. fine $100/28.5 grams or less); CONN. GEN. STAT. ANN. §21a-279a (max. fine $150/ less than .5 oz.); ME. REV. STAT. ANN. tit. 22 §2383[1][A](max. fine $600/1.25 oz. or less); MASS. GEN. LAWS ANN. ch. 94C §32L (max. fine $100/1 oz. or less); MINN. STAT. ANN. §§152.027[subd.4(a)], 152.01 [subd. 16] (max fine $200/42.5 grams or less); MISS. CODE ANN. §41-29-139(c)(2)(A); NEB. REV. STAT. §28-416(13)(a) (max. fine $300/1 oz. or less); NEV. REV. STAT. §453.336[4](max. fine $600/1 oz. or less); N.Y. PENAL LAW §130.35; N.C. GEN. STAT. §§90-95(d)(4)(maxs. $200 fine—10 days imprisonment/.5 oz. or less); OHIO REV. CODE ANN. §§2925.11(C)(3), 2929.28(A)(2)(a)(v)(max. fine $150/100 grams or less); ORE. REV. STAT. §475.864(3)(max. fine $650/1 oz. or less); R.I. GEN. LAWS §21-28- 4.01(c)(2)(iii)(max. fine $150/1 oz. or less); VT. STAT. ANN. tit.18 §4230a (max. fine $200/1 oz. or less).

[49] ALASKA STAT. §§17.37.010 to 17.37.080; ARIZ. REV. STAT. ANN. §§36-2801 to 36-2819; CAL. HEALTH & SAFETY CODE §§11362.5 to 11362.9; CONN. GEN. STAT. ANN. §§21a-408 to 21a-408q; COLO. REV. STAT. ANN. §§12-43.3-101 to 12-43.3-1102; DEL. CODE ANN. tit.16 §§4901A to 4926A; D.C. CODE §§7-1671.01 to 7-1671.13; HAWAII REV. STAT. §329-121 to 329-128; 410 ILL. COMP. STAT. ANN. §§130/10 to 130/140; ME. REV. STAT. ANN. tit. 22 §§2421 to 2430-B; MASS. GEN. LAWS ANN. ch. 94C App. §§1-1 to 1-17; MICH. COMP. LAWS ANN. §§333.26421 to 333.26430; MONT. CODE ANN. §50-46-301 to 50-46-344; NEV. REV. STAT. §§453A.010 to 453A.810; N.H. REV. STAT. ANN. §§126-X:1 to 126-X:11; N.J. STAT. ANN. §§24:61-1 to 24:61-16; N.MEX. STAT. ANN. §§26-2B-1 to 26-2B-7; ORE. REV. STAT. §§475.300 to 475.346; R.I. GEN. LAWS §21-28.6-1 to 21-28.6-13; VT. STAT. ANN. tit.18 §§4471 to 4474l; WASH. REV. CODE ANN. §69-51A.005 to 69-51A.903. The Supreme Court in Oakland Cannabis Buyers' Cooperative held that the federal Controlled Substances Act does not contain an implicit medical marijuana exception, United States v. Oakland Cannabis Buyers' Cooperative, 532 U.S. 483, 495 (2001).

[50] COLO. REV. STAT. ANN. §§12-43.3-101 to 12-43.3-1102; WASH. REV. CODE ANN. §§69-50.325 to 69-50.369.

[51] 309 F.3d 629 (9th Cir. 2002).

[52] Id. at 632.

[53] 21 §823(f)("The Attorney General shall register practitioners (including pharmacies ...) to dispense ... controlled substances.... The Attorney General may deny an application for such registration ... [in] the public interest. In determining the public interest, the following factors shall be considered: ... (4) Compliance with applicable State, Federal, or local laws relating to controlled substances....").

[54] Id. at 636 (internal citations omitted).

[55] Id. (emphasis in the original).

[56] Id. at 636-39.

[57] ALASKA STAT. §§17.37.010 to 17.37.080; ARIZ. REV. STAT. ANN. §§36-2801 to 36-2819; CAL. HEALTH & SAFETY CODE §§11362.5 to 11362.9; CONN. GEN. STAT. ANN. §§21a-408 to 21a-408q; COLO. REV. STAT. ANN. §§12-43.3-101 to 12-43.3-1102; DEL. CODE ANN. tit.16 §§4901A to 4926A; D.C. CODE §§7-1671.01 to 7-1671.13; HAWAII REV. STAT. §§329-121 to 329-128; 410 ILL. COMP. STAT. ANN. §§130/10 to 130/140; ME. REV. STAT. ANN. tit. 22 §§2421 to 2430- B; MASS. GEN. LAWS ANN. ch. 94C App. §§1-1 to 1-17; MICH. COMP. LAWS ANN. §§333.26421 to 333.26430; MONT. CODE ANN. §§50-46-301 to 50-46-344; NEV. REV. STAT. §§453A.010 to 453A.810; N.H. REV. STAT. ANN. §§126-X:1 to 126-X:11; N.J. STAT. ANN. §§24:6I-1 to 24:6I-16; N.MEX. STAT. ANN. §§26-2B-1 to 26-2B-7; ORE. REV. STAT. §§475.300 to 475.346; R.I. GEN. LAWS §§21-28.6-1 to 21-28.6-13; VT. STAT. ANN. tit.18 §§4471 to 4474l; WASH. REV. CODE ANN. §§69-51A.005 to 69-51A.903.

[58] ALASKA STAT. §17.37.030; ARIZ. REV. STAT. ANN. §36-2811; CAL. HEALTH & SAFETY CODE §§11362.71(e), 11362.765, 11362.775; CONN. GEN. STAT. ANN. §§21a-408a to 21a-408c; DEL. CODE ANN. tit.16 §4903A; D.C. CODE §7-1671.02; HAWAII REV. STAT. §329-122; 410 ILL. COMP. STAT. ANN. §130/25; ME. REV. STAT. ANN. tit. 22 §§2423-A to 2423-D; MASS. GEN. LAWS ANN. ch. 94C App. §§1-4, 1-5; MICH. COMP. LAWS ANN. §333.26424; MONT. CODE ANN. §50-46-319; NEV. REV. STAT. §453A.310; N.H. REV. STAT. ANN. §126-X:2; N.J. STAT. ANN. §24:6I-6; N.MEX. STAT. ANN. §26-2B-4; ORE. REV. STAT. §§475.316, 475.319; R.I. GEN. LAWS §21-28.6-8; VT. STAT. ANN. tit.18 §4474b; WASH. REV. CODE ANN. §69-51A.030.

[59] ARIZ. REV. STAT. ANN. §36-2801[3].

[60] E.g., DEL. CODE ANN. tit. 16 §4902A(3)[b]("... severe, debilitating pain, that has not responded to previously prescribed medication or surgical measures for more than 3 months or for which other treatment options produced serious side effects....").

[61] E.g., CONN. GEN. STAT. ANN. §21a-408(10); D.C. CODE §7-1671.01(19); MICH. COMP. LAWS ANN. §333.264246(a)(6); MONT. CODE ANN. §50-46-307(1)(d); N.H. REV. STAT. ANN. §126-X:1[X], [XVI]; N.J. STAT. ANN. §24:6I-3; N.MEX. STAT. ANN. §26-2B-3 [G]; R.I. GEN. LAWS §21-28.6-3(10); VT. STAT. ANN. tit.18 §4472(12); but see NEV. REV. STAT. §453A.364 (recognition of nonresident cards).

[62] E.g., ALASKA STAT. §17.37.040(a)(4)(1 oz.); DEL. CODE ANN. tit.16 §4903A(a)(6 oz.); D.C. CODE §7-1671.03(a)(2 oz.); 410 ILL. COMP. STAT. ANN. §130/10(a)(1), 130/25(a)(2.5 oz.); ME. REV. STAT. ANN. tit. 22 §§2423-A[1][A](2.5 oz.); MICH. COMP. LAWS ANN. §333.26424(2.5 oz.); MONT. CODE ANN. §50-46-319 (1 oz.); NEV. REV. STAT. §453A.200 (1 oz.); N.H. REV. STAT. ANN. §126-X:2[I](2 oz.); ORE. REV. STAT. §475.320 (24 oz.); R.I. GEN. LAWS §21- 28.6-4 (2.5 oz.).

[63] E.g., ALASKA STAT. §17.37.040(a)(2); CONN. GEN. STAT. ANN. §21a-408a(b)(2); DEL. CODE ANN. tit.16 §4904A(3); D.C. CODE §7-1671.03; 410 ILL. COMP. STAT. ANN.

§130/30(3)(F); MICH. COMP. LAWS ANN. §333.26427(b)(3)(B); N.H. REV. STAT. ANN. §126-X:3[II](c); N.MEX. STAT. ANN. §26-2B-5[A](3)(d); ORE. REV. STAT. §§475.316(1)(b).

[64] E.g., ALASKA STAT. §17.37.010(e); ARIZ. REV. STAT. ANN. §36-2804.02; CONN. GEN. STAT. ANN. §21a-408b; DEL. CODE ANN. tit.16 §4909A; 410 ILL. COMP. STAT. ANN. §130/55; ME. REV. STAT. ANN. tit. 22 §§2425; MASS. GEN. LAWS ANN. ch. 94C App. §1-1; MONT. CODE ANN. §50-46-308; NEV. REV. STAT. §453A.210; N.H. REV. STAT. ANN. §126-X:4; N.J. STAT. ANN. §24:6I-4; N.MEX. STAT. ANN. §26-2B-7; ORE. REV. STAT. §§475.309, 475.312; R.I. GEN. LAWS §21-28.6-4; VT. STAT. ANN. tit.18 §4474.

[65] E.g., ARIZ. REV. STAT. ANN. §36-2811; CAL. HEALTH & SAFETY CODE §§11362.77, 11362.775; CONN. GEN. STAT. ANN. §21a-408b; DEL. CODE ANN. tit.16 §4903A; 410 ILL. COMP. STAT. ANN. §130/25; MASS. GEN. LAWS ANN. ch. 94C App. §§1-4, 1-5; MICH. COMP. LAWS ANN. §333.26424; MONT. CODE ANN. §50-46-319; NEV. REV. STAT. §453A.200; N.H. REV. STAT. ANN. §126-X:2; N.J. STAT. ANN. §24:6I-6; N.MEX. STAT. ANN. §26-2B-4; ORE. REV. STAT. §§475.316, 475.319; R.I. GEN. LAWS §21-28.6-8; VT. STAT. ANN. tit.18 §4474b.

[66] E.g., ALASKA STAT. §17.37.030; HAWAII REV. STAT. §329-122; MICH. COMP. LAWS ANN. §333.26424; ORE. REV. STAT. §§475.316, 475.319; R.I. GEN. LAWS §21-28.6-8.

[67] E.g., ARIZ. REV. STAT. ANN. §36-2804; CAL. HEALTH & SAFETY CODE §11362.8; CONN. GEN. STAT. ANN. §21a-408h; DEL. CODE ANN. tit.16 §4914A; D.C. CODE §7-1671.06; HAWAII REV. STAT. §329-122; 410 ILL. COMP. STAT. ANN. §§130/85 to 130/130; ME. REV. STAT. ANN. tit. 22 §2428; MASS. GEN. LAWS ANN. ch. 94C App. §§1-9; MONT. CODE ANN. §§50-46-308, 5-46-309; NEV. REV. STAT. §§453A.320 to 453A.344; N.H. REV. STAT. ANN. §126-X:8; N.J. STAT. ANN. §24:6I-7; N.MEX. STAT. ANN. §26-2B-7; ORE. REV. STAT. §475.304; VT. STAT. ANN. tit.18 §4474g.

[68] Washington Initiative 502 at §20, amending RCW 69.50.4013 and 2003 c 53 s 334, available at http://sos.wa.gov/ _assets/elections/initiatives/i502.pdf.

[69] Id. at §15.

[70] Id. at §21.

[71] Id. at §4.

[72] Id.

[73] Joel Millman, Washington State Sets Pot-Sales Rules, WALL ST. JOURNAL, October 16, 2013.

[74] Washington State Liquor Control Board, Marijuana Licenses, Application Process, Requirements, and Reporting, at https://lcb.app.box.com/adopted-rules.

[75] Id. at 20-21.

[76] Washington Initiative 502 at §26.

[77] Id. §31.

[78] Steve Elliot, Toke Signals: Washington Waits While Colorado Buys, SEATTLE WEEKLY, December 30, 2013.

[79] See Bob Young, In Washington, Pot Business Applications Surpass 3,000, SEATTLE TIMES, December 24, 2013 (noting that "[s]tate investigators plan to evaluate growing licenses first, so crops can be started as soon as possible in hopes of supplying retail stores by May [2014]".).

[80] Jake Ellison, Where Legal Marijuana Stands on the Brink of the New Year, SEATTLE POST INTELLIGENCER, December 30, 2013, at http://blog.seattlepi.com/marijuana/2013/12/30/where-legal-marijuana-stands-on-the-brink-of-the-newyear/#14194101=0; see also Jack

Healy, Up Early and in Line for a Marijuana Milestone in Colorado, N.Y. TIMES, January 1, 2014 ("While Colorado has incorporated the existing medical marijuana system, Washington is starting from scratch, with all production and sale of legal recreational marijuana linked to a new system of licenses, which will not be issued until late February or early March.").

81 Colorado Amendment 64, Amending Colo. Const. Art. XVIII §16(3), available at http://www.colorado.gov/cs/Satellite?blobcol=urldata&blobheader=application/pdf&blobkey=id&blobtable=MungoBlobs&blobwhere= 1251834064719&ssbinary=true.

82 Id.

83 Id.

84 Id. at §16(4).

85 Id. at §16(5)(f). See also Dan Frosch, Colorado Localities Make Own Rules Before Final Decision on Marijuana Sales, N.Y. TIMES, June 12, 2013; John Ingold, Colorado Marijuana Stores Likely to be Concentrated in Few Cities, THE DENVER POST, July 25, 2013.

86 See Jake Ellison, City/County Bans, Moratoriums, and Zoning Approvals for Marijuana Businesses in Washington, SEATTLE POST INTELLIGENCER, December 12, 2013, at http://blog.seattlepi.com/marijuana/2013/12/12/bansmoratoriums-and-zoning-approvals-for-marijuana-businesses-as-far-as-we-know/#18853101=0&18413103=0; Gene Johnson, No Welcome Yet for Pot Shops in Many Wash. Cities, SEATTLE POST INTELLIGENCER, January 1, 2014.

87 The licensing and regulatory systems envisioned by both Colorado and Washington are modeled on similar state alcohol distribution schemes found across the country.

88 Task Force Report on the Implementation of Amendment 64, March 13, 2013 at 9, available at http://www.colorado.gov/cms/forms/dor-tax/A64TaskForceFinalReport.pdf.

89 Id. at 16-19.

90 Id. at 28-31.

91 Id. at 33.

92 Id. at 49-51.

93 See Colorado Dep't of Revenue, Permanent Rules Related to the Colorado Retail Marijuana Code, September 9, 2013, available at http://www.colorado.gov/cs/Satellite? Blobcol =urldata&blobheadername1=Content-Disposition&blobheadername2=Content-Type& blobheadervalue1= inline%3B+filename%3D%22Retail+Marijuana+Rules%2C+Adopted+090913%2C+Effective+101513.pdf%22& blobheadervalue2=application%2Fpdf&blobkey=id&blobtable=MungoBlobs&blobwhere= 1251888487553&ssbinary= true.

94 Id.

95 Id.

96 Colorado Legislative Council Staff, Fiscal Impact Statement: Proposition AA, Retail Marijuana Taxes, September 24, 2013, available at http://www.leg.state.co.us/LCS/Initiative%20Referendum/1314initrefr.nsf/b74b3fc5d676cdc987257ad8005bce6a/e3e37fa33a36873887257b6c0077ac93/$FILE/ Retail%20Marijuana%20Taxes_FN.pdf.

97 John Ingold, Colorado Issues First Licenses for Recreational Marijuana Businesses, DENVER POST, December 23, 2013.

98 Id.

99 Jack Healy, Up Early and in Line for a Marijuana Milestone in Colorado, N.Y. TIMES, January 1, 2014.

[100] United States v. Goodwin, 457 U.S. 368, 380 (1982).

[101] Wayte v. United States, 470 U.S. 598, 607 (1985).

[102] Memorandum for selected U.S. Attorneys from David W. Ogden, Deputy Attorney General, Investigations and Prosecutions in States Authorizing the Medical Use of Marijuana, October 19, 2009 (hereinafter Ogden Memorandum) available at http://www.justice.gov/opa/documents/medical-marijuana.pdf.

[103] Id. at 1-2.

[104] Id. at 3.

[105] Todd Grabarsky, Conflicting Federal and State Medical Marijuana Policies: A Threat to Cooperative Federalism, 116 W.VA. L. REV. 1, 3 (2013)("While the Ogden Memo reaffirmed the illegality of all forms of medical marijuana at the federal level, it made clear that the federal executive policy with regards to medical marijuana permissible at the state level would be for the most part hands-off."); Karen O'Keefe, State Medical Marijuana Implementation and Federal Policy, 16 J. HEALTH CARE L & POL'Y 39, 51 (2013)("On October 19, 2009, Deputy Attorney General David Ogden issued a memorandum memorializing the new federal policy.... This memo was widely interpreted as meaning that the federal government would not be targeting medical marijuana providers."); Sam Kamin & Eli Wald, Marijuana Lawyers: Outlaws or Crusaders? 91 ORE. L. REV. 869, 881 (2013)("In states that had adopted [Medical Marijuana] provisions, the memo was seen as a green light to the open sale of marijuana."); Alex Kreit, Reflections on Medical Marijuana Prosecutions and the Duty to Seek Justice, 89 DENV. U. L. REV. 1027, 1037 (2012)("The New York Times ran a front-page article about the memo under the headline U.S. Won't Prosecute in States That Allow Medical Marijuana reporting that '[p]eople who use marijuana for medical purposes and those who distribute it to them should not face federal prosecution, provided they act according to state law, the Justice Department said Monday in a directive with far-reaching political and legal implications.'").

[106] Gerald Caplan, Medical Marijuana: A Study of Unintended Consequences, 43 MCGEORGE L. REV. 127, 130, 136-37 (2012)("Statewide, more than 70% of doctors recommendations were written by fewer than 15 physicians in Colorado, and severe or chronic pain, a catchall category, accounted for ninety-four percent of all reported conditions.... [In] Oregon, fewer than ten percent of the roughly 35,000 patients holding cards suffered from cancer, multiple sclerosis, glaucoma, or the o0ther specific debilitating conditions cited in the legislation. Ninety percent of registered cardholders cited chronic pain as their qualifying debilitating disease. Nevada's percentages are nearly identical. Montana's are slightly lower, with seventy-one percent of all medical marijuana users suffering from chronic pain.").

[107] Alex Kreit, The Federal Response to State Marijuana Legalization: Room for Compromise, 91 ORE. L. REV. 1029, 1036 n.33 (2013).

[108] Id.

[109] Id. at 135.

[110] Michael Vitiello, Joints or the Joint: Colorado and Washington Square Off Against the United States, 91 ORE. L.REV. 1009, 1015 (2013).

[111] Memorandum for U.S. Attorneys from James M. Cole, Deputy Attorney General, Guidance Regarding the Ogden Memo in Jurisdictions Seeking to Authorize Marijuana for Medical Use, June 29, 2011 (hereinafter Cole 2011 Memorandum), available at http://www.justice.gov/oip/docs/dag-guidance-2011-for-medical-marijuana-use.pdf.

[112] Id. at 2.

[113] Sam Kamin & Eli Wald, Marijuana Lawyers: Outlaws or Crusaders? 91 ORE. L. REV. 869, 881-83 (2013)("In the fall of 2011, California's four Untied States Attorneys announced

that a federal grand jury had returned indictments against several marijuana cooperative owners throughout the state, charging them with violations of the CSA. In addition, the United States Attorneys sent cease and desist letters to both dispensary owners and their landlords, giving them forty-five days to move their operations or else face arrest. In addition to the clear threat of criminal prosecution, this action made clear that the threat of civil enforcement—explicit in the Cole memo—was not an empty one. For a federal government with limited enforcement resources, the specter of civil forfeiture is an incredibly powerful tool. Similar crackdowns have since taken place in Washington state, Colorado, and Montana.").

[114] See e.g., Montana Caregivers Association, LLC v. United States, 841 F.Supp.2d 1147, 1148 (D.Mont. 2012)("The plaintiffs describe themselves as 'caregivers: growers and distributors of medical marijuana to qualified patients within the State of Montana.' They filed their complaint after federal authorities raided their facilities in March 2011 and seized live marijuana plants, dried marijuana, and related equipment. The plaintiffs claim the raids were unlawful because (1) Montana law allowed them to grow and produce marijuana for medical consumption and (2) the United States Department of Justice represented that they would not actively prosecute medical marijuana caregivers."); United States v. Washington, 887 F.Supp.2d 1077, 1090-91 (D. Mont. 2012)("All of the pending motions to dismiss on estoppel grounds rely on the common underlying principle that the federal government, having stated several times that it would not initiate federal drug prosecutions of sellers or users of medical marijuana acting in compliance with the laws of their respective states, should now be estopped from pursuing this federal prosecution in contradiction of those statements. The most prominent of the federal government's various pronouncements on the topic of medical marijuana is what has become known as the 'Ogden memo.'").

[115] Memorandum for U.S. Attorneys from James M. Cole, Deputy Attorney General, Guidance Regarding Marijuana Enforcement, August 29, 2013 (hereinafter Cole 2013 Memorandum), available at http://www.justice.gov/iso/opa/ resources/3052013829132756857467.pdf.

[116] See, e.g., New York Times Editorial, A Saner Approach on Drug Laws, N.Y. TIMES, September 1, 2013.

[117] See, e.g., Wall Street Journal Editorial, The Beltway Choom Gang, WALL ST. J., September 5, 2013.

[118] Cole 2013 Memorandum, at 1-2.

[119] Id. at 2-3.

[120] Id. at 3.

[121] Cole 2011 Memorandum, at 1-2.

[122] Cole 2013 Memorandum, at 3.

[123] See discussion supra pp. 14-19.

[124] Emerald Steel Fabricators, Inc., v. Bureau of Labor and Industries, 348 Ore. 159, 230 P.3d 518 (2010).

[125] For more information about this topic, see CRS Report WSLG682, Banking Difficulties for State-Legalized Marijuana Dispensaries, by M. Maureen Murphy; see also Reuters, Easier Pot Policy Won't Relieve Dispensaries' Banking Woes, CNBC.com, September 5, 2013, at http://www.cnbc.com/id/101011966; Serge F. Kovaleski, Banks Say No to Marijuana Money, Legal or Not, N.Y. TIMES, January 11, 2014.

[126] Memorandum for U.S. Attorneys from James M. Cole, Deputy Attorney General, Guidance Regarding Marijuana Related Financial Crimes, February 14, 2014 (hereinafter Cole 2014 Memorandum), available at http://www.justice.gov/usao/wae/news/2014/2014-02-14-FinCin.html.

[127] U.S. CONST., Art. VI, cl. 2.

[128] See discussion of preemptive effect of treaties infra.

[129] Northern States Power Co. v. Minnesota, 447 F.2d 1143, 1145 (8th Cir. 1971).

[130] See, e.g., Mutual Pharmaceutical Co., Inc. v. Bartlett, 133 S.Ct. 2466, 2473 (2013)("Under the Supremacy Clause, from which our pre-emption doctrine is derived, any state law, however clearly within a State's acknowledged power, which interferes with or is contrary to federal law, must yield.").

[131] Arizona v. United States, 132 S.Ct. 2492, 2501 (2012)("[T]he States are precluded from regulating conduct in a field that Congress, acting within its proper authority, has determined must be regulated by its exclusive governance. The intent may be inferred from a framework of regulation so pervasive ... that Congress has left no room for the states to supplement it or where there is a federal interest ... so dominant that the federal system will be assumed to preclude enforcement of state laws on the same subject.").

[132] Hillman v. Maretta, 133 S.Ct. 1943, 1950 (2013).

[133] Arizona v. United States, 132 S.Ct. at 2501.

[134] Hillman v. Maretta, 133 S.Ct. 1943, 1950 (2013).

[135] Section 708 of the Controlled Substances Act (21 U.S.C. §903).

[136] See, e.g., County of San Diego v. San Diego NORML, 165 Cal.App. 4th 798 (2008)(holding that a state law conflicts with the CSA only where it is impossible to comply with both the state and federal law).

[137] 2013 Colo.App. LEXIS 1971 (December 19, 2013).

[138] Id. at *4.

[139] Id. at *11.

[140] Id. at *4 ("We consider County of San Diego well-reasoned and follow it here.")

[141] County of San Diego v. San Diego NORML, 165 Cal.App. 4th 798 (2008).

[142] 2013 Colo.App. LEXIS 1971 at *4.

[143] Id. at *5.

[144] County of San Diego v. San Diego NORML, 165 Cal.App.4th at 808.

[145] Id. at 826. The court also found that the California law was not vulnerable to impossibility preemption since the CSA did not outlaw the issuance of the medical marijuana cards that the California law required. Thus, it was not impossible for an individual to honor both the CSA and the California card law. Id. at 819-21.

[146] 2014 Mich. LEXIS 194, at *2-*4 (Mich. 2014).

[147] Id. at *23.

[148] Id. at *11-*12.

[149] Id. at *17.

[150] Emerald Steel Fabricators, Inc. v. Bureau of Labor and Industries, 230 P.3d 518 (2010).

[151] Id. at 529 ("To be sure, state law does not prevent the federal government from enforcing its marijuana laws against medical marijuana users in Oregon if the federal government chooses to do so. But the state law at issue in Michigan Canners did not prevent the federal government from seeking injunctive and other relief to enforce the federal prohibition in that case. Rather, state law stood as an obstacle to the enforcement of federal law in Michigan Canners because state law affirmatively authorized the very conduct that federal law prohibited, as it does in this case"), citing, Michigan Canners & Freezers Association v. Agricultural Marketing and Bargaining Bd., 467 U.S. 461 478 (1984).

[152] Id. at 529.

[153] Willis v. Winters, 253 P.3d 1058, 1064 n.6 (2011). In Willis, the court held that the federal statute that outlawed firearm possession by a user of controlled substances did not preempt

the Oregon statute that authorizes sheriffs to issue "concealed carry" permits to otherwise qualified applications who were users of medical marijuana. Id. at 1065- 66.

[154] In re: Rent-Rite Super Kegs West Ltd., 484 B.R. 799 (Dec 19, 2012). Whether the debtor was engaged in criminal activity was an issue in the case because "a federal court cannot be asked to enforce the protections of the Bankruptcy Code in aid of a Debtor whose activities constitute a continuing federal crime." Id. at 805.

[155] Id. at 805 ("The fact that there is a difference in legislative philosophy creates no conflict that requires an analysis of federal preemption under the Supremacy Clause."). Part of the confusion over the proper application of obstacle preemption to state marijuana laws may stem from an apparent disagreement over the nature of the obstacle that is required to trigger preemption. As previously noted, the Supreme Court has held that a state law is preempted when it "stands as an obstacle to the accomplishment and execution of the full purposes and objectives of Congress." Most courts that have rejected preemption challenges to state medical marijuana laws have interpreted "the full purposes and objectives of Congress" in relation to the federal government's ability to enforce federal law. As such, these courts have generally held that because the state law does not create a shield or otherwise immunize state residents from federal criminal prosecutions, the law does not constitute an obstacle to "the enforcement of federal law." To the contrary, the Oregon Supreme Court reasoned that the fact that the state law in no way inhibited federal prosecutions did not mean that the law did not otherwise create an obstacle to the Congress's chief objective in enacting the CSA; that of curtailing drug use.

[156] Gonzales v. Raich, 545 U.S. 1, 5, 22 (2005)(The question presented in this case is whether the power vested in Congress by Article I, §8, of the Constitution, '[t]o make all Laws which shall be necessary and proper for carrying into Execution' its authority to 'regulate Commerce with foreign Nations, and among the several States' includes the power to prohibit the local cultivation and use of marijuana in compliance with California law.... Given the enforcement difficulties that attend distinguishing between marijuana cultivated locally and marijuana grown elsewhere, ... we have no difficulty concluding that Congress had a rational basis for believing that failure to regulate the intrastate manufacture and possession marijuana would leave a gaping hole in the CSA. Thus, as in Wickard, ... Congress was acting well within its authority to 'make all Laws which shall be necessary and proper' to 'regulate Commerce ... among the several States.'").

[157] New York v. United States, 505 U.S. 144, 161 (1981)("Congress may not commandeer the legislative process of the States by directly compelling them to enact and enforce a regulatory program."). Printz v. United States 521 U.S. 898, 935 (1997)("The Federal Government may [not] ... command the States' officers, or those of their political subdivisions, to administer or enforce a federal regulatory program.").

[158] United States v. Washington, 887 F.Supp.2d 1077, 1101 (D.Mont. 2012); United States v. Stacy, 696 F.Supp.2d 1141, 1145 (S.D.Cal. 2010); Raich v. Gonzales, 500 F.3d 850, 867 n.17 (9th Cir. 2007).

[159] Sacramento Nonprofit Collective v. Holder, 855 F.Supp.2d 1100, (E.D.Cal. 2012)("[I]s is well established under United States Supreme Court authority that if a power is delegated to Congress in the Constitution, the Tenth Amendment expressly disclaims any reservation of that power to the States. Since the power to regulate the intrastate possession, manufacturing, and distribution of marijuana is delegated to Congress through the Commerce Clause, Raich I, 545 U.S. at 15, [the] allegation that the power to regulate marijuana in California was reserved to California through the Tenth Amendment is

foreclosed by United States Supreme Court precedent."). Montana Caregivers Association, LLC v. United States, 841 F.Supp.2d 1147, 1149-150 (D.Mont. 2012)(to the same effect).

160 U.S. Const. amend. X (emphasis added)("The powers not delegated to the United States by the Constitution, nor prohibited by it to the States, are reserved to the States respectively, or to the people."). Amend. IX ("The enumeration in the Constitution, of certain rights, shall not be construed to deny or disparage others retained by the people."). Amend. V ("No person shall ... be deprived of life, liberty, or property without due process of law...."). Amend. XIV, §1 ("... No State shall ... deprive any person of life, liberty, or property without due process of law....").

161 Cf., Raich v. Gonzales, 500 F.3d 850, (9th Cir. 2007)("The Supreme Court held in Gonzales v. Raich that Congress acted within the bounds of its Commerce Clause authority when it criminalized the purely intrastate manufacture, distribution, or possession of marijuana in the Controlled Substances Act, See 125 S.Ct. at 2215. Thus, after Gonzales v. Raich, it would seem that there can be no Tenth Amendment violation in this case.").

162 Washington v. Glucksberg, 521 U.S. 702, 721 (1997)(internal citations omitted).

163 Raich v. Gonzales, 500 F.3d at 861-66; United States v. Fry, 787 F.2d 903, 905 (4th Cir. 1986); United States v. Fogarty, 692 F.2d 542, 547 (8th Cir. 1982); Marin Alliance for Medical Marijuana v. Holder, 866 F.Supp.2d 1142, 1156-157 (N.D.Cal. 2011); Kuromiya v. United States, 37 F.Supp.2d 717, 725-27 (E.D.Pa. 1999).

164 United States v. Washington, 887 F.Supp.2d 1077, (D.Mont. 2012)("Estoppel by official misleading statement ... applies where the defendant had a reasonable belief that his conduct was sanctioned by the government. [It] requires the accused to show that (1) an authorized government official, empowered to render the claimed erroneous advice, (2) who has been made aware of all the relevant historical facts, (3) affirmatively told him the proscribed conduct was permissible, (4) that he relied on the false information, and (5) that his reliance was reasonable. The Defendants assert the defense of estoppel by official misleading statement based on the Ogden memo; statements made to the press or to Congress by then-presidential-candidate Barack Obama, his campaign spokesman, his White House spokesman, and United States Attorney General Eric Holder; the characterizations of those statements in news media; the government's entry into the stipulation in Santa Cruz; and statements made to at least one Defendant by Flathead Tribal Police drug investigator Arlen Auld. None of these statements justifies dismissal on a theory of estoppel by official misleading statement."); Marin Alliance for Medical Marijuana v. Holder, 866 F.Supp.2d at 1155-156; Sacramento Nonprofit Collective v. Holder, 855 F.Supp.2d 1100, 1111-112 (E.D.Cal. 2012); United States v. Stacy, 696 F.Supp.2d 1141, 1146-148 (S.D.Cal. 2012); United States v. Schafer, 625 F.3d 629, 637-38 (9th Cir. 2010). The Second Circuit has rejected the contention that the Ogden memo constituted a rescheduling of marijuana, United States v. Canori, 737 F.3d 181, 184-85 (2d Cir. 2013).

165 United States v. Washington, 887 F.Supp.2d at 1102-103 ("The Ninth Circuit squarely rejected a rational basis challenge to the classification of marijuana as a schedule I substance in United States v. Miroyan, 5577 F.2d 489, 495 (9th Cir. 1978). Although Fleming argues that since Miroyan, additional studies and changes in state law have called into question the rationality of Congress' policy, there remains sufficient debate regarding the public benefits and potential for harmful consequences of marijuana use to find a rational basis to uphold the continued classification of marijuana as a schedule I controlled substance."); Marin Alliance for Medical Marijuana v. Holder, 866 F.Supp.2d at 1146-147 ("There is no right under the Constitution to have a law go unenforced against you, even if you are the first person against whom it is enforced, and even if you think (or can prove)

you are not as culpable as some others who have gone unpunished. The law does not need to be enforced everywhere to be legitimately enforced somewhere")(responding to plaintiffs' equal protection challenge that prosecutors' threatened to take legal action against them as the landlords of marijuana dispensaries' but visited so similar threats upon the landlords of Colorado dispensaries); Sacramento Nonprofit Collective v. Holder, 855 F.Supp.2d at 1109-110 (same equal protection challenge; same result).

[166] Beek v. City of Wyoming, 2014 Mich. LEXIS 194 (Mich. 2014)(Michigan Medical Marihuana Act precludes any absolute municipal ban on cultivating marijuana within city limits); City of Riverside v. Inland Empire Patients Health and Wellness Center, Inc., 300 P.3d 494, 499 (Cal. 2013)(City may use its municipal powers to ban marijuana dispensaries within the city); Giuliani v. Jefferson County Board of County Commissioners, 303 P.3d 131, 135 (Colo.App. 2012)(municipal officials may ban the cultivation or sale of marijuana within the county).

[167] Santa Barbara Patients' Collective Health Cooperative v. City of Santa Barbara, 911 F.Supp. 884, 892-93 (C.D.Cal. 2012)(pre-ordinance permit holder enjoyed a vested right to operate a marijuana dispensary that could not be curtailed without due process of law); Conejo Wellness Center, Inc. v. City of Agoura Hills, 214 Cal.App.4th 1534, 1562 (2013) (pre-ordinance dispensary operator had no vested liberty right requiring procedural due process to extinguish).

[168] See e.g., Deirdre Fernandes, Banks Shun Fledgling Marijuana Firms in Mass, THE BOSTON GLOBE ("Elsewhere in the country, legal marijuana businesses have run into the same problems ... Some marijuana businesses have found ways to get a bank account by, for example, setting up separate holding companies that avoid any reference in the names to marijuana. Even then, once banks get a whiff of where the money comes from, they close the accounts"), available at http://www.bostonglobe.com/business/2014/01/29/medical-marijuana-firms-face-cash-economy-bankssteer-clear/88ftUTUbcaYvZfA7fpuENN/story.htm. Legal Marijuana Market Exceeds Tax Hopes, Creating Opportunities, MARKETWATCH ("The Denver Post reported Wednesday that banks holding commercial loans on properties that lease to Colorado marijuana businesses say they don't plan to refinance those loans when they come due. Banks say property used as collateral for those loans theoretically is subject to federal drug-seizure laws, which makes the loans a risk. Colorado's two largest banks, Wells Fargo Bank and First Bank, say they won't offer new loans to landowners with preexisting leases with pot businesses. And Wells Fargo and Vestra Bank have told commercial loan clients they either have to evict marijuana business or seek refinancing elsewhere."), available at http://www. Market watch.com/story/legal-marijuana-market-exceeds-tax-hopes-creating-opportunities-2014-02- 27?/reflink=MW-news-stmp.

[169] 2014 Cole Memorandum; Department of the Treasury, Financial Crimes Enforcement Network, BSA Expectations Regarding Marijuana-Related Business, FIN-2014-G001 (Feb. 14, 2014)(herein after FinCEN guidance), available at http://www.fincen/gov/ sstatutes_ regs/guidance/pdf/FIN-2014-G002.pdf.

[170] 21 U.S.C. §5318(g); 31 C.F.R. §1020.320.

[171] 31 U.S.C. §5322.

[172] 31 U.S.C. §5324(d).

[173] 31 U.S.C. §5318(h); 12 U.S.C. §1818(s); 12 U.S.C. §1786(q)(1).

[174] 31 C.F.R. §§1020.200-1020.220.

[175] 31 U.S.C. §5313; 31 C.F.R. subpt.1020C; 31 C.F.R. subpt.1010 C.

[176] 31 U.S.C. §5322.

[177] 31 U.S.C. §5324(d).

[178] 18 U.S.C. §1957(a), (d).

[179] 18 U.S.C. §1956(a)(1)(A)(i).

[180] 18 U.S.C. §1956(a)(1).

[181] 18 U.S.C. §1957(a).

[182] 18 U.S.C. §1956(h).

[183] 18 U.S.C. §2. E.g., United States v. Lyons, 740 F.3d 702, 715 (1st Cir. 2014)(internal citations omitted)("An aider and abettor is punishable as a principal if, first, someone else actually committed the offense and, second, the aider and abettor became associated with the endeavor and took part in it, intending to ensure its success. The central requirement for the second element is a showing that the defendant consciously shared the principal's knowledge of the underlying criminal act, and intended to help the principal.").

[184] 18 U.S.C. §§981(a)(1)(A), 982(a)(1).

[185] 12 U.S.C. §1818.

[186] This presumably does not include enterprises, gangs, or cartels that possess or distribute marijuana in violation of the CSA but in compliance with applicable state law.

[187] This would seem to serve as a warning to interstate marijuana tourists and the businesses that serve them.

[188] Given the value of the product, violence may be an inescapable attribute of marijuana cultivation and sale, see e.g., Benjamin B. Wagner & Jared C. Dolan, Medical Marijuana and Federal Narcotics Enforcement in the Eastern District of California, 43 MCGEORGE L. REV. 109, 121 (2012).

[189] Id. at 122 ("About seventy percent or more of marijuana eradicated in California every year comes from public lands."); Marijuana Crops in California Threaten Forests and Wildlife, The New York Times, available at http://www.nytimes.com/2013/06/21/us/marijuana-crops-in-california-threaten-forests-and-wildlife.html.

[190] FinCEN guidance, at 2.

[191] Id. at 3-4.

[192] Id. at 4.

[193] Id. at 4-5.

[194] Id. at 5-7.

[195] Id. at 7.

[196] See, generally, Matthew D. Macy, Employment Law and Medical Marijuana, 41 COLORADO LAWYER 57 (2012).

[197] Coats v. Dish Network, LLC, 303 P.3d 147 (Colo.App. 2013); Casias v. Wal-Mart Stores, Inc., 695 F.3d 428 (6th Cir. 2012); Emerald Steel Fabricators, Inc. v. Bureau of Labor and Industries, 230 P.3d 518 (Ore. 2010); Ross v. RagingWire Telecommunications, Inc., 42 Cal.4th 920 (2008).

[198] Casias v. Wal-Mart Stores, Inc., 695 F.3d at 435 (internal citations omitted)(emphasis in the original)("[T]he MMMA [Michigan Medical Marihuana Act] does not regulate private employment; [r]ather the Act provides a potential defense to criminal prosecution or other adverse action by the state.... MMMA contains no language stating that it repeals the general rule of at-will employment in Michigan or that it otherwise limits the range of allowable private decisions by Michigan businesses"); Emerald Steel Fabricators, Inc. v. Bureau of Labor and Industries, 230 P.3d at 169 n.7, citing, Roe v. TeleTech Customer Car Management, 152 Wash.App. 388, 216 P.3d 1055 (2009); Ross v. RagingWire Telecommunications, 42 Cal.4th 920 (2008) ("Both the California and Washington courts have held that, in enacting their states' medical marijuana laws, the voters did not intend to

affect an employer's ability to take adverse employment actions based on the use of medical marijuana.").

[199] Coats v. Dish Network, LLC, 303 P.3d at 149-53 (The Colorado Civil Rights Act (CCRA) outlaws firing employees for "lawful" out of work activities. Use of marijuana as permitted by the Colorado medical marijuana but in violation of the CSA was not a lawful activity for purposes of the CCRA); Emerald Steel Fabricators, Inc. v. Bureau of Labor and Industries, 230 P.3d at 535 (Because the employee was fired for illegal use of marijuana under the CSA, the state employment discrimination statute, modelled after the ADA, does not apply); see also, James v. City of Lake Forest, 700 F.3d 394, 397 n.3 (9th Cir. 2012)("[T]he ADA does not protect medical marijuana users who claim to face discrimination on the basis of their marijuana use.").

[200] Maryland v. King, 133 S.Ct. 1958, 1969 (2013)(internal citations and quotation marks omitted)("In giving content to the inquiry whether an intrusion is reasonable, the Court has preferred some quantum of individualized suspicion ... as a prerequisite to a constitutional search or seizure. But the Fourth Amendment imposes no irreducible requirement of such suspicion. In some circumstances, such as when faced with special law enforcement needs, diminished expectations of privacy, minimal intrusions, or the like, the Court has found that certain general, or individual circumstances may render a warrantless search or seizure reasonable."). See, generally, CRS Report R42326, Constitutional Analysis of Suspicionless Drug Testing Requirements for the Receipt of Governmental Benefits, by David H. Carpenter.

[201] 50 U.S.C. §3343(b)("After January 1, 2008, the head of a Federal agency may not grant or renew a security clearance for a covered person who is an unlawful user of a controlled substance ...); 50 U.S.C. §3343(a)(2)("The term covered person means : (A) an officer or employee of a Federal Agency; (B) a member of the Army, Navy, Air Force, or Marine Corps who is on active duty or is in an active status; and (C) an officer or employee of a contractor of a Federal Agency"); e.g., 51 U.S.C. §31102(b)("(1) Employees of administration.-The Administrator shall establish a program applicable to employees of the Administration whose duties include responsibility for safety-sensitive, security, or national security functions. Such program shall provide for preemployment, reasonable suspicion, random, and post-accident testing for use, in violation of applicable law or Federal regulation, of alcohol or a controlled substance.... (2) Employees of contractors.-The Administrator shall, in the interest of safety, security, and national security, prescribe regulations. Such regulations shall establish a program that requires Administration contractors to conduct preemployment, reasonable suspicion, random, and post-accident testing of contractor employees responsible for safety-sensitive, security, or national security functions (as determined by the Administrator) for use, in violation of applicable law or Federal regulation, of alcohol or a controlled substance.... (3) Suspension, disqualification, or dismissal.-In prescribing regulations under the programs required by this subsection, the Administrator shall require, as the Administrator considers appropriate, the suspension, disqualification, or dismissal of any employee to which paragraph (1) or (2) applies, in accordance with the provisions of this section, in any instance where a test conducted and confirmed under this section indicates that such employee has used, in violation of applicable law or Federal regulation, alcohol or a controlled substance."). See also, 49 U.S.C. §20140(Program of required preemployment, reasonable suspicion, random, and post-accident testing of all railroad employees responsible for safety-sensitive functions).

[202] Barrett v. Claycomb, 705 F.3d 315, 322 (8th Cir. 2013), referring to cases collected in, Kreig v. Seybold, 481 F.3d 512,518 (7th Cir. 2007).

[203] 41 U.S.C. §§8101 et seq.

[204] 41 U.S.C. §§8102, 8103; 2 C.F.R. pt.182; 48 C.F.R. §§23.500 et seq.; 48 C.F.R. §2.101 (simplified acquisition threshold). U.S. Dept. of Labor, Drug-Free Workplace Act of 1988 Requirements, available at http://www.dol.gov/ elaws/asp/drugfree/screenr.htm.

[205] 41 U.S.C. §§8102, 8103. There are slightly different requirements for individuals and organizations that receive federal contracts or grants. 41 U.S.C. §§8102, 8103. See U.S. Dept. of Labor, Drug-Free Workplace Act of 1988 Requirements for Individuals, available at http://www.dol.gov/elaws/asp/drugfree/req_ind.htm ("Any individual who receives a contract or grant from the Federal government, regardless of dollar value, must agree not to engage in the unlawful manufacture, distribution, dispensation, possession or use of a controlled substance in the performance of this contract/grant."), and U.S. Dept. of Labor, Drug-Free Workplace Act of 1988 Requirements for Organizations, available at http://www.dol.gov/elaws/asp/drugfree/require.htm ("All organizations covered by the Drug-Free Workplace Act of 1988 are required to provide a drug-free workplace by ... [publishing] and [giving] a policy statement to all covered employees informing them that the unlawful manufacture, distribution, dispensation, possession or use of a controlled substance is prohibited in the covered workplace and specifying the actions that will be taken against employees who violate the policy).

[206] Due to their potential impact on public safety, commercial pilots, truckers, bus drivers and the like are subject to periodic drug testing which the United States Department of Transportation has recently made clear does not excuse a positive drug test for either medical or recreational marijuana use, U.S. Department of Transportation, Fact Sheet: DOT 'Medical" Marijuana Notice (Feb. 23, 2013), citing 49 C.F.R. 40.151, available at http://www.dot/gov/odapc/medicalmarijuana-notice ("The Department of Justice (DOJ) issued guidelines for Federal prosecutors in states that have enacted laws authorizing the use of 'medical marijuana.' We have had several inquiries about whether the DOJ advice to Federal prosecutors regarding pursing criminal case will have an impact upon the Department of Transportation's longstanding regulation about the use of marijuana by safety-sensitive transportation employees—pilots, school bus drivers, truck drivers, train engineers, subway operators, aircraft maintenance personnel, transit fire-armed security personnel, ship captains, and pipeline emergency response personnel, among others. We want to make it perfectly clear that the DOJ guidelines will have no bearing on the Department of Transportation's regulated drug testing program. We will not change our regulated drug testing program based upon these guidelines to Federal prosecutors."). DOT issued a similar notice with regard to recreational marijuana, U.S. Department of Transportation, DOT 'Recreational' Marijuana Notice (Feb. 22, 2013), available at http://www.dot.gov/odapc/dot-recreational-marijuana-notice.

[207] See, generally, A Cruel Choice: Patients Forced to Decide Between Medical Marijuana and Employment, 26 HOFSTRA LAB. & EMP. L.J. 619 (2008).

[208] E.g., R.I. GEN. LAWS §22-28.6-4(c)("No school, employer or landlord may refuse to enroll, employ or lease to or otherwise penalize a person solely for his or her status as a cardholder."); Ariz. Rev. Stat. Ann. §36-2813[B](("Unless a failure to do so would cause an employer to lose a monetary or licensing related benefit under federal law or regulations, an employer may not discriminate against a person in hiring, termination or imposing any term or condition of employment or otherwise penalize a person based upon either: 1. The person's status as a cardholder. 2. A registered qualified patient's positive drug test for

marijuana components or metabolites, unless the patient used, possessed or was impaired by marijuana on the premises of the place of employment or during the hours of employment.").

[209] Casias v. Wal-Mart Stores, Inc., 695 F.3d at 435; Emerald Steel Fabricators, Inc. v. Bureau of Labor and Industries, 230 P.3d at 169 n.7, citing, Roe v. TeleTech Customer Car Management, 152 Wash.App. 388, 216 P.3d 1055 (2009); Ross v. RagingWire Telecommunications, 42 Cal.4th 920 (2008).

[210] Under some state laws, eligibility for unemployment compensation turns on proof the marijuana use occurred on the job or had job-related consequences, Compare, Peace River Distributing, Inc. v. Florida Unemployment Appeals Commission, 80 So.3d 461, 464 (Fla.App. 2012)(discharged employee who tested positive for marijuana use was not entitled to unemployment compensation); Virginia Employment Commission v. Community Alternatives, Inc., 705 S.E.2d 530, (Va.App. 2011)(same); Maskerines v. Unemployment Compensation Board of Review, 13 A.3d 553, 560 (Pa.Comm. 2011)(employer need not show job nexus where discharged employee had agreed to comply with employer's drug free policy); Division of Employment Security v. Comer, 199 S.W.3d 915, 921 (Mo.App. 2006); with, Johnson v. So Others Might Eat, Inc., 53 A.3d 323, (D.C.App. 2012); Cusack v. Williams, 286 S.W.3d 180, 182 (Ark.App. 2008)(employer need not show job nexus where bus driver's off duty marijuana use made him ineligible for the commercial driver's license, a reasonable condition of employment). See also, Desilet v. Glass Doctor, 132 P.3d 412, 415-16 (Idaho 2006)(off-duty marijuana use is presumed job-related if the employer followed state approved testing guidelines; otherwise the employer must show a job nexus).

[211] I.R.C. §§61, 63, 26 U.S.C. §§61, 63.

[212] James v. United States, 366 U.S. 213, 218-20 (1961); United States v. Renner, 648 F.3d 680, 686-87 (8th Cir. 2011);

[213] I.R.C. §162, 26 U.S.C. §162.

[214] I.R.C. §280E, 26 U.S.C. §280E. See also, Oliver v. Commissioner, 139 T.C. 19 (Aug. 2, 2012)(merchant may also unable to subtract the cost of goods sold under some circumstances).

[215] I.R.S. Gen. Couns. Mem. 2011-0005 (Mar. 25, 2011), available at http://www.irs.gov/ pub/irs-wd/11-0005.pdf.

[216] Section 213 of the Internal Revenue Code allows taxpayers to deduct certain uncompensated medical expenses. The regulations make clear, however, that they may not deduct illegal treatments, 26 C.F.R. §1.213-1(e)(ii). Although the IRS has indicated that the uncompensated costs of herbs prescribed by a physician are deductible, it is at best unclear whether the advice can be understood to include marijuana whose possession is unlawful under the CSA. See, I.R.S. Gen. Couns. Mem. 2010-0080 (June 25, 2010), available at http://www.irs.gov/pub/irs-wd/10-0080.pdf.

[217] 18 U.S.C. §§922(g)(3), 924(a)(2).

[218] 27 C.F.R. §478.11.

[219] See Open Letter to All Federal Firearm Licensers, September 21, 2011, available at http://www.atf.gov/files/press/releases/2011/09/092611-atf-open-letter-to-all-ffls-mari juana-for-medicinal-purposes.pdf.

[220] 18 U.S.C. §924(c), 21 U.S.C. §841.

[221] 18 U.S.C. §§924(c)(1)(A)(i) to (iii), 2. Co-conspirators are subject to imprisonment for not more than 20 years, 18 U.S.C. §924(o).

[222] 42 U.S.C. §§13661-13662. See, generally, Medical Marijuana and the Effect of State Laws on Federally Subsidized Housing, 57 WAYNE L. REV. 1437 (2011).

[223] 42 U.S.C. §§13661-13662.

[224] Id.

[225] Memorandum from Helen R. Kanoovsky, Medical Use of Marijuana and Reasonable Accommodation in Federal Public and Assisted Housing, January 20, 2011, available at http://www.scribd.com/doc/47657807/HUD-policy-Memo-on-Medical-Marijuana-in-Public-Housing. See also, Assenberg v. Anacortes Housing Authority, 268 Fed.Appx. 643 (9th Cir. 2008)(Under the Fair Housing Act, tenant in publicly assisted housing is not entitled to medical necessity defense and termination of lease based on tenant's drug use did not violate HUD policy).

[226] In Labron v. Secretary, Florida Department of Children and Family, 710 F.3d 1202, 1211-214 (11th Cir. 2013), the U.S. Court of Appeals upheld, on Fourth Amendment grounds, a challenge to a state requirement that applicants for Temporary Assistance for Needy Families (TANF) benefits submit to drug testing.

[227] A second Rule, Rule 8.4(b) provides that, "it is professional misconduct for a lawyer to ... (b) commit a criminal act that reflects adversely on the lawyer's honesty, trustworthiness, or fitness as a lawyer in other respects." See, generally, Sam Kamin & Eli Wald, Marijuana Lawyers: Outlaws or Crusaders? 91 OR. L. REV. 869 (2013).

[228] In some states, bar association ethics opinions are a service provided to members of the bar and as a general rule are only available to them. This and the rapidly evolving nature of the issue suggest the possibility of other opinions.

[229] State Bar of Arizona Ethics Opinion 11-01 (Feb. 2011), available at http://www.azbar.org/Ethics/EthicsOpinions/ ViewEthicsOpinion?id=710.

[230] "• If a client or potential client requests an Arizona lawyer's assistance to undertake the specific actions that the [Arizona medical marijuana] Act expressly permits; and • The lawyer advises the client with respect to the potential federal law implications and consequences thereof or, if the lawyer is not qualified to do so, advises the client to seek other legal counsel regarding those issues and limits the scope of his or her representation; and • The client, having received full disclosure of the risks of proceeding under the state law, wishes to proceed with a course of action specifically authorized by the Act; then • The lawyer ethically may perform such legal acts as are necessary or desirable to assist the client to engage in the conduct that is expressly permissible under the Act."

[231] Maine Professional Ethics Commission, Opinion #199 (July 7, 2010), available at http://www.mebaroverseers.org/ attorney_services/opinion.html?id=110134.

[232] Connecticut Bar Association, Professional Ethics Committee, Informal Opinion 2013-20 (Jan. 16, 2003), available at http://www.ctbar.org/userfiles/Comittees/Professional Ethics/ Opinions/Informal_Opinion_2013-02.pdf.

[233] Colorado Bar Association Ethics Committee, Formal Opinion 125 (Oct. 21, 2013), 42 COLO. LAWYER 19 (Dec. 2013).

[234] Here, the Opinion finds support in 21 U.S.C. §885(d) which affords federal, state, and local law enforcement officers immunity for enforcement of federal, state, and local controlled substance laws.

[235] Rule 8.6. Counseling Clients Concerning Marijuana

"Notwithstanding any other provision of these Rules, a lawyer shall not be in violation of these rules or subject to discipline for counseling or assisting a client to engage in conduct that, by virtue of (1) Article XVIII, Miscellaneous, Section 14, Medical Use of Marijuana for Persons Suffering From Debilitating Medical Conditions, or (2) Article XVII,

Miscellaneous, Section 16, Personal Use and Regulation of Marijuana, the lawyer reasonably believes to be either permitted or within an affirmative defense to prosecution under state criminal law, and which the lawyer reasonably believes is in compliance with legislation or regulations implement such provisions solely because that same conduct, standing alone, may violate federal criminal law."

[236] King County Bar Association, KCBA Ethics Advisory Opinion on I-502 & Rules of Professional Conduct (Oct. 2013), available at http://www.kcba.org/judicial/legislative/pdf/i502_ethics_advisory_opinion_october_2013.pdf.

[237] Washington State Bar Association, Committee on Professional Ethics, Proposed Advisory Opinion 2232 (Jan. 8, 2014) The proposed comment would state, "Since the passage of I-502 by Washington voters in November 2012, both the federal and state government have devoted considerable resources to allowing I-502 [relating to recreational marijuana] to come into effect without regard to federal controlled substances laws, as long as certain stated federal concerns regarding matters such as sales to minors and other unlawful conduct are addressed. See e.g., Washington State Bar Association Advisory Opinion 2232 and sources cited. At least until there is a subsequent change of federal enforcement policy, a lawyer who counsels or assists a client regarding conduct permitted under I-502 does not, without more, violate RPC 1.2(d). See also Washington Comment [7] to RPC 8.4 [related criminal acts committed by attorneys]," available at http://www.kcba.org/judicial/legislative/pdf/wsba_response_011514.pdf.

[238] Proposed Advisory Opinion 2232. The proposed comment to accompany Rule 8.4 would state: ":A unique circumstance was presented by the November 2012 passage by Washington voters of I-502, which allows for the creation of a state-regulated system for the production and sale of marijuana for recreational purposes. At least until there is a subsequent change of federal enforcement policy, a lawyer who engages in conduct permitted under I-502, does not, without more, violate RPC 8.4(g), (i), (k), or (n). See also Washington Comment [18] at RPC 1.2."

[239] 21 U.S.C. §823(f).

[240] Id.

[241] Id.

[242] See, The DEA Position on Marijuana, April 2013, available at http://www. justice. gov/dea/docs/marijuana_position_2011.pdf. Researchers have reportedly encountered difficulties obtaining the marijuana necessary for their research. See e.g., Gardiner Harris, Researchers Find Study of Medical Marijuana Discouraged, N.Y. Times, January 18, 2010.

[243] 21 U.S.C. §823(a). In evaluating whether granting a registration is in the "public interest" the Attorney General must consider:

maintenance of effective controls against diversion of particular controlled substances and any controlled substance in schedule I or II compounded therefrom into other than legitimate medical, scientific, research, or industrial channels, by limiting the importation and bulk manufacture of such controlled substances to a number of establishments which can produce an adequate and uninterrupted supply of these substances under adequately competitive conditions for legitimate medical, scientific, research, and industrial purposes;

compliance with applicable State and local law;

promotion of technical advances in the art of manufacturing these substances and the development of new substances;

prior conviction record of applicant under Federal and State laws relating to the manufacture, distribution, or dispensing of such substances;

past experience in the manufacture of controlled substances, and the existence in the establishment of effective control against diversion; and such other factors as may be relevant to and consistent with the public health and safety.

With respect to the CSA's reference to the nation's "obligations under international treaties," the Single Convention on Narcotic Drugs establishes that "any signatory nation that 'permits the cultivation of [marijuana or opium]' must designate one or more agencies to: license cultivators and designate where plants may be grown; purchase and take physical possession of each year's crops; and have the exclusive right of importing, exporting, wholesale trading and maintaining stocks other than those held by manufacturers of opium alkaloids, medicinal opium or opium preparations." Craker v. DEA, 714 F.3d 17, 20 (1st Cir. 2013).

244 Craker v. DEA, 714 F.3d 17, 20 (1st Cir. 2013).

245 See, NIDA's Role in Providing Marijuana for Research, http://www.drugabuse.gov/drugs-abuse/marijuana/nidasrole-in-providing-marijuana-research.

246 H.R. 499, §101(a).

247 Id. §102.

248 Id. §103.

249 27 U.S.C. §§201 et seq.

250 Id. §201, adding new 27 U.S.C. §301.

251 Id. §301.

252 Id. §302.

253 H.R. 501, §2(a), adding new 26 U.S.C. §5901.

254 The bill defines "marijuana enterprise" as a producer, importer, manufacturer, distributor, retailer, or any person who transports, stores, displays, or otherwise participates in any business activity that handles marijuana or marijuana products. Id. §2(a), adding new 26 U.S.C. §5904(8).

255 Id. §2(a), adding new 26 U.S.C. §5911.

256 Id. §2(a), adding new 26 U.S.C. §5912.

257 Id. §2(a), adding new 26 U.S.C. §§5921, 5922.

258 H.R. 689, §2(a)(1).

259 Id. §2(a)(2).

260 21 U.S.C. §§301 et seq.

261 H.R. 689, §§2(b), (3).

262 Id. §4.

263 Id.

264 H.R. 710, §2(a), adding new 18 U.S.C. §§3436(a), (b)(1).

265 §2(a), adding new 18 U.S.C. §3436(c).

266 Id. §2(a), adding new 18 U.S.C. §3436(b)(2).

267 21 U.S.C. §881.

268 H.R. 784, §3, amending Section 511(a) of the CSA (21 U.S.C. §881(a)(7)).

269 H.R. 964, §2, amending Section 708 of the CSA (21 U.S.C. §903).

270 H.R. 2652, §3(a).

271 Id. at §3(c).

272 Id. at §5, amending 31 U.S.C. §5318(g).

273 Id. at §2.

In: Marijuana
Editor: Victor P. Tyson

ISBN: 978-1-63482-057-8

Chapter 2

FEDERAL PROPOSALS TO TAX MARIJUANA: AN ECONOMIC ANALYSIS*

Jane G. Gravelle and Sean Lowry

SUMMARY

The combination of state policy and general public opinion favoring the legalizing of marijuana has led some in Congress to advocate for legalization and taxation of marijuana at the federal level. The Marijuana Tax Equity Act of 2013 (H.R. 501) would impose a federal excise tax of 50% on the producer and importer price of marijuana. The National Commission on Federal Marijuana Policy Act of 2013 (H.R. 1635) proposes establishing a National Commission on Federal Marijuana Policy that would review the potential revenue generated by taxing marijuana, among other things.

This report focuses solely on issues surrounding a potential federal marijuana tax. First, it provides a brief overview of marijuana production. Second, it presents possible justifications for taxes and, in some cases, estimates the level of tax suggested by that rationale. Third, it analyzes possible marijuana tax designs. The report also discusses various tax administration and enforcement issues, such as labeling and tracking.

* This is an edited, reformatted and augmented version of a Congressional Research Service publication R43785, prepared for Members and Committees of Congress dated November 13, 2014.

Economic theory suggests the efficient level of taxation is equal to marijuana's external cost to society. Studies conducted in the United Kingdom (UK) and Canada suggest that the costs of individual marijuana consumption to society are between 12% and 28% of the costs of an individual alcohol user, and total social costs are even lower after accounting for the smaller number of marijuana users in society. Based on an economic estimate of $30 billion of net external costs for alcohol, the result is an external cost of $0.5 billion to $1.6 billion annually for marijuana. These calculations imply that an upper limit to the economically efficient tax rate could be $0.30 per marijuana cigarette (containing an average of one half of a gram of marijuana) or $16.80 per ounce. An increased number of users in a legal market would raise total costs, but not necessarily costs per unit.

Some could also view excise taxes as a means to curtail demand, particularly as the price of marijuana can be expected to drop from current retail prices of up $200-$300 per ounce to prices closer to the cost of production at $5-$18 per ounce, if broadly legalized. The demand for marijuana is estimated to be relatively price inelastic, meaning that consumer demand is relatively insensitive to price changes. Although previous studies of marijuana demand largely examine consumers willing to engage in illegal activities, it appears that higher tax rates would have a minor effect on reducing demand. With this said, tax policy, coupled with adequate law enforcement, could be an effective tool to limit marijuana consumption among youth, as empirical studies indicate that their demand is more sensitive to price than non-youth.

Excise taxes on marijuana could also be levied primarily to raise revenue, as has been historically the case with tobacco and alcohol. As an illustration, assuming a total market size of $40 billion, a federal tax of $50 per ounce is estimated to raise about $6.8 billion annually, after accounting for behavioral effects associated with price decreases following legalization.

The choices in administrative design could affect consumer behavior, production methods, evasion rates, or the tax base of a federal marijuana excise tax. Some of the more significant choices include whether to exempt medicinal uses or homegrown marijuana from tax.

INTRODUCTION

The cultivation, distribution, and possession of marijuana are prohibited for any reason other than to engage in federally approved research under the federal Controlled Substances Act of 1970 (CSA; P.L. 91-513). Yet, 23 states, the District of Columbia, and Guam have passed legislation or initiatives legalizing qualified sale, possession, manufacture, and distribution of medical marijuana, and 17 states and the District of Columbia have decriminalized the possession of marijuana.[1] In addition, in November 2012, Colorado and Washington became the first states to legalize, regulate, and tax small amounts of marijuana for non-medicinal use (so-called recreational) by individuals 21 and older. Commercial sales of recreational marijuana became legal in the state of Colorado beginning on January 1, 2014—the first jurisdiction in the world to do so. Washington's commercial marijuana market opened on July 7, 2014. On November 4, 2014, Alaska and Oregon became the third and fourth states to approve ballot initiatives to legalize, regulate, and tax marijuana for recreational purposes.[2] That same day, the District Columbia approved further measures to legalize the cultivation, possession, and exchange (but not the commercial sales) of marijuana.[3]

In addition to state and local movements to decriminalize or legalize the production, sales, or use of marijuana, there has been a general shift in popular sentiment toward marijuana policy. According to polls conducted by Rassmussen, the Pew Research Center, and Gallup, a majority of Americans favor legalizing marijuana.[4]

The combination of state policies and general sentiment has led to heightened debate over the merits of marijuana legalization at the federal level. For example, in the 113th Congress, bills have been introduced that would remove marijuana from the list of Schedule I drugs prohibited by the Controlled Substances Act and impose a federal excise tax on the production and importation of marijuana.[5] Another bill proposes the establishment of a National Commission on Federal Marijuana Policy that would review the potential revenue generated by taxing marijuana, among other things.[6] Overall, the debate concerning marijuana legalization is complex, as it spans across issues ranging from criminal justice to public health and safety. The revenue-raising potential of a marijuana tax could become a contributing factor in the desirability of legalizing marijuana.

This report focuses solely on one aspect of the economic debate over federal marijuana legalization: imposing an excise tax on legalized marijuana.[7] First, it provides a brief overview of marijuana production. Second, it presents possible arguments for taxes and, in some cases, estimates the level of tax suggested by that rationale. Third, possible marijuana tax designs are analyzed.[8]

A BRIEF OVERVIEW OF MARIJUANA PRODUCTION

Marijuana is a preparation of the plant, *Cannabis sativa*, generally used as a recreational drug or medicine primarily for its psychoactive and physiological effects.[9] The term *marijuana* refers to the dried leaves and flowers of the cannabis plant. The main psychoactive ingredient in marijuana is delta-9-tetrahydrocannabinol (THC). THC is the primary cannabinoid responsible for the "high" that users experience when consuming the drug. Still, THC is only one of many "cannabinoid" chemical compounds in marijuana that contribute to the effects of the psychoactive effects of marijuana (in terms of strength, onset, duration, etc.). Consumers could desire different strains of marijuana for the contents of other cannabinoids that do not produce a psychoactive effect. For example, marijuana strains high in cannabidiol (CBD) are often sought to provide relief from anxiety.[10]

Depending on its preparation, the potency, or relative concentration, of a particular product derived from marijuana can vary. The stalks and stems of a marijuana plant have almost no psychoactive content, whereas the leaves and flowers (buds) of the plant have increasing concentrations of THC. The hair-like trichomes on the buds are coated with a translucent resin that contains the highest concentration of THC on the plant. Marijuana plants are also either male or female. If female plants are grown in controlled environments, separate from pollination of male plants, then the female plants are capable of growing buds that produce more resin. This process is used to grow *sinsemilla* (Spanish for without seed) varieties of marijuana, which typically contain 10%-18% THC content (about three times the level of conventional, commercial-grade marijuana derived from pollinated plants).[11]

Marijuana consumption methods vary. Marijuana is generally consumed by smoking the dried plant matter. A "joint" is made by rolling marijuana in cigarette paper whereas a "blunt" is made by hollowing some or all of the tobacco from a cigar and replacing it with marijuana. Although smoking habits vary by user, a typical joint contains less than half a gram of marijuana, and each "hit" or drag on the joint contains approximately one-twentieth of a gram of marijuana.[12] Numerous other devices for consuming marijuana exist, ranging from glass pipes to vaporizers (which heat the chemicals in marijuana, but avoid creating the smoke irritants associated with combustion).

Cannabis can also be processed into a number of different products, all with their own THC concentration levels and typical methods of consumption. For example, hashish or "hash" is made by pressing trichomes together into a brick-shaped product with more than 40% THC content.[13] THC is also capable of being dissolved in fats, oils, and alcohol for use in the creation of "edibles," such as candy or baked goods.[14]

Why a Federal Excise Tax on Marijuana?

Economic analysis as a general rule suggests that excise taxes are less desirable than more general taxes (such as income or broad based sales taxes) because they distort prices of different commodities. This section discusses several possible reasons for imposing an excise tax on marijuana: (1) reflect external, or spillover, costs to society; (2) discourage use, particularly for youth; (3) prevent too rapid a fall in price; (4) fund related programs; and (5) raise revenue.

Taxes to Reflect External Costs

Economic efficiency occurs when the price of a commodity (at the margin) equals its costs. If consumption of marijuana imposes costs on others, then the consumer cost is too small and economic efficiency could be achieved by imposing a tax equal to consumption cost. This rationale has often been used for similar commodities, such as alcohol and tobacco.[15]

In considering this justification and the level of tax economic analysis suggests, the external costs should be separate from the costs the user bears. For example, if a substance causes early death, the value of the lost years of life and the individual's own costs in treating illness falls on the individual. Society bears the loss of tax revenue from those lost earnings and some of the costs of treating illness that fall on private or social health insurance. However, society also receives gains from the early death in the amount of smaller health costs and transfer payments (such as Social Security) in the future. These future costs should be discounted. At least in studies of other substances, these external costs are typically much smaller than the total costs.[16] A 1991 study by Manning et al. used this method to estimate the external costs of alcohol and tobacco.[17] Adjusting these estimates for price changes, those results imply a cost of $30 billion for alcohol, which will be used to estimate the cost for marijuana, for which no study of this nature exists.[18] As with the case of tobacco, these external costs are typically much smaller than the total costs.

Although no U.S. study of marijuana of this nature could be located, it is possible to investigate the likely magnitude of a tax necessary to correct for externalities of marijuana use by examining studies that compare the costs of cannabis use to alcohol.

A British study ranked different drugs by harm on a scale of 1 to 100.[19] Overall, alcohol ranked 72, whereas cannabis ranked 20, or 28% of alcohol. Considering just the external harm, alcohol ranked 47 and cannabis ranked 9, or 19% of alcohol. A Canadian study found an even smaller ratio of health costs per user, about 12%.[20] It is also likely that the non-health costs of marijuana are lower than for alcohol. For example, part of the spillover effect of alcohol is in the effect of traffic accidents, but studies tend to find that marijuana impairs driving ability less than alcohol.[21]

Evidence also suggests that smoking marijuana is inversely related to domestic violence.[22] The Canadian study found larger enforcement costs for marijuana, but that effect is probably due to marijuana's illicit status. (For additional discussion of some of the various social effects of marijuana, see *Appendix A*.)

In addition to indications that the externalities of marijuana are smaller per user than alcohol, the prevalence of marijuana use is smaller. According to the National Survey of Drug Use and Health (NSDUH), alcohol usage in 2013 for the population 12 and older was 66.3% in the past year and 52.2% in the past month, whereas marijuana usage was 12.6% and 7.5% respectively.[23] Thus marijuana usage is 19% (based on use in the past year) and 14% (based on use in the past month) as common as alcohol usage. These numbers suggest that the external costs of marijuana range from $0.5 billion to $1.7 billion.[24]

To translate this amount into a tax per ounce requires an estimate of the total market size and the price. A 2014 report issued by the White House Office of National Drug Control Policy (ONDCP) provides estimates of the unit price, total expenditure, and total consumption weight of marijuana in the United States.[25] The calculations extrapolate from two sets of data: (1) the NSDUH, which is a self-reported survey of drug use habits; and (2) survey data from drug-offense arrestees in a limited number of areas designated as Arrestee Drug Abuse Monitoring (ADAM) jurisdictions.[26] The report finds that from 2002 to 2010, the amount of marijuana consumed in the United States likely increased by about 40%.[27] The ONDCP report also provides estimates of $30 billion, $41 billion, and $60 billion (given various assumptions) for total U.S. expenditures on marijuana in 2010.[28] Additionally, the report indicates that THC levels in marijuana increased from 2000 to 2010.[29]

Using the ONDCP estimates of the market cited above ($30 billion to $60 billion), the estimates of external cost imply a tax of 0.8% to 5.3% of current price.

The White House's 2014 ONDCP report provides estimates of the price per gram of marijuana from 2000 to 2010. The nominal price of marijuana is roughly constant over the period, implying the inflation-adjusted price of marijuana was likely decreasing over time. In 2010, the White House report estimates that the price per gram of marijuana was $7.11 per gram ($199.08 per ounce), not accounting for differences in quality.

In addition, there are anecdotal prices recorded through anonymous sources and informal interviews with consumers or dealers in the underground market. Other researchers have used different techniques and newer data sources to estimate the price of marijuana across a wider range of locations. One website, priceofweed.com, contains anonymous, volunteer-submitted data on individual transactions across a variety of global locations, down to the level of particular towns or cities. Using data from priceofweed.com, the price of marijuana can be estimated as $317 per ounce, after weighting the observations for the quality of marijuana reported.[30] However, it is unclear if data submitted to priceofweed.com are representative. Anecdotal reports in the media indicate that high-quality marijuana can be obtained in some areas, such as Washington State, for $28 per eighth of an ounce ($224 per ounce, but presumably less if bought in bulk).[31] Another source suggests that consumers would have to pay at least $10 per gram, or $238 per ounce.[32]

Tax rates ranging from 0.8% to 5.3% of the price might seem small to some, but marijuana prices are currently much higher than the production cost because of the illicit nature of the market. In a legal market, prices would be lower. These estimates of external cost range from $1.60 to $16.80 per ounce. The smaller estimate assumes a 0.8% tax and a $200 price; and the larger estimate assumes a 5.3% tax and a $317 price. Estimates discussed in subsequent sections suggest the price in a fully competitive market could be as low as $5 per ounce, so that the tax would be greater relative to price.

If a typical joint contains a half of a gram of marijuana, then the largest estimate is the equivalent of $0.30 per joint. For comparison, the federal tax on cigarettes is $0.05 for each cigarette whereas taxes on alcoholic drinks range from $0.04 for a five ounce glass of wine, $0.05 for a 12 ounce beer, and $0.13 for a 1.5 ounce shot of distilled spirits.[33] Thus, the tax on a joint would be about the same as the tax on a six-pack of beer. States (and sometimes localities) also impose taxes on alcohol and tobacco, and they presumably would also tax marijuana as Colorado and Washington have.[34] These state taxes are probably already in excess of the external costs of marijuana.

Although clearly many uncertainties surround attempts to measure the external costs of marijuana (as reflected in the range of estimates), the information that is available suggests a relatively small tax compared with current prices.

Discouraging Use, Including among Youth

An argument can be made for imposing a tax to discourage marijuana users because these potential consumers underestimate long-term health costs and possible dependence when they begin to use the substance. This argument may be particularly important to underage use of marijuana.

Some disagree that marijuana is physically addictive, although it may result in dependence. A recent study found that about 9% of marijuana users become dependent.[35] Another study found that medical marijuana laws in the United States increase the probability of marijuana abuse or dependency by 15%-27% among adults aged 21 or older.[36]

Information on the risks of marijuana could be improved with more research and dissemination of the results of that research. In the case of the risk of addiction or dependence, economists disagree on whether the behavior of users is suboptimal, at least in the case of adults. “Rational addiction” theories indicate that as long as consumers are informed they are making desirable choices.[37]

Other economists argue that individuals can be engaged in hyperbolic discounting, in which they make time-inconsistent choices in the present that their future selves would not prefer.[38]

An important issue in determining a tax that is intended for the best interests of the potential user is that the tax would also reduce income. If the purpose of the tax is to increase the user’s welfare, that benefit must be offset by the reduced income. Individuals that typically consume multiple joints per day consume a disproportionate share of the marijuana used in the United States (a trend similar to alcohol use) and in heavier doses. Researchers have estimated that 20% of marijuana users constitute about 80% of consumption.[39] Like taxes on alcohol and tobacco, the majority of the burden of a marijuana tax would fall primarily on the heaviest users.[40]

A tax on marijuana, like most excise taxes, is likely to be regressive, and this outcome might be considered undesirable (although current users are likely to benefit from a decline in price from making marijuana legal).

Evaluating the potential benefit to users of imposing taxes to discourage consumption depends on how users' participation in the market and the quantity purchased respond to the tax. It is assumed that the tax is passed on in price.[41] Responses to price changes are generally expressed as elasticities by economists: the percentage change in quantity divided by the percentage change in price. For example, if the elasticity is -0.5, a 10% increase in price leads to a 5% decrease in quantity consumed. If the price elasticity is low, the tax alters behavior very little, while imposing a significant tax burden, and users are harmed by the tax although their small change in consumption may be closer to the optimal choice (i.e., the choice they would make fully accounting for the costs).

Gallet (2014) examines a combination of 42 studies on the demand for various illicit drugs, 13 of which measure the price elasticity demand of marijuana.[42] After controlling for various factors related to the studies, Gallet's model predicts elasticities of demand for marijuana ranging between -0.15 and -0.31. In other words, a 1% increase in the price of marijuana results in a 0.15% to 0.31% decrease in the demand for marijuana. Consumer demand is relatively unresponsive to changes in price.[43] Thus, it is more likely that users would be harmed overall by a tax imposed for their own benefit, because gains in moving to more optimal consumption may be more than offset by lost income from the tax.[44]

Government policy is often focused on limiting use of drugs (whether legal or illegal) by minors. Current, state marijuana legalization laws disallow purchases by those under 21 years old, but, as with other commodities, youth may still obtain them in various ways. Estimates of the price elasticity for minors tend to be larger. One study had an overall estimate of -0.44 but an estimate of -1.01 for ages 12-17 years old.[45] Thus taxes may be more effective in reducing usage among youth (assuming these youth are not purchasing marijuana through illegal markets or acquiring legally produced marijuana through informal, secondary channels without cost).

The policy question then may be how much of a tax burden should be placed on non-responsive adult users to limit consumption of youth. (A similar issue arises with taxation of tobacco.) This question has no quantifiable answer, but one objective that might be considered is to set the tax so that the price of marijuana does not fall substantially with legalization and expanded demand, especially among minors who are more responsive to price. The next section discusses the potential level of such a tax.

Capturing the Current Differential between Cost and Price

The characteristics of a legalized, and low-cost, marijuana market, as well as the concerns discussed above about youth consumption, may suggest a tax to keep these prices from falling precipitously until the consequences of a legal market can be determined. Depending on those consequences, a relatively high tax may be retained, or the tax may be reduced.

After legalization, it is estimated that the cost of marijuana will decrease significantly because more will be produced and the implicit costs of evading law enforcement will decline. Many producers are currently confined to smaller-scale or indoor operations that lack economies of scale. Workers in the illicit trade of marijuana must also be compensated more than comparable workers in industries that are not subject to law enforcement risk (e.g., laborers harvesting fruits or vegetables). Although a legalized market for marijuana could develop in such a way that some firms are able to attain market power and charge higher prices for their particular brands of marijuana compared with generic brands, the market for marijuana could become more competitive. In a competitive market, firms earn no profit above the normal return necessary to attract capital (if they did, other firms would enter to exploit it).[46] Prices would, therefore, fall to reflect lower production costs.

The difference between the projected cost in a legal competitive market and current prices (which largely reflect illicit production) provides a range within which a federal tax rate might be considered, at least initially. The tax should not be set too high (including any state and local taxes) to encourage illicit productions, so that this approach might be aimed at offsetting only part of the price reduction expected from the legalization of marijuana.

Caulkins (2010) estimates the costs of producing and processing legalized marijuana, under a number of methods and scenarios.[47] As shown in *Table* **1**, Caulkins estimates that the production cost *per pound* of high-quality marijuana would be roughly equivalent to the current retail price *per ounce*. Outdoor production of marijuana is estimated to cost substantially less, per pound of output. However, marijuana cultivated outdoors is less likely to contain the higher levels of THC found in plants grown indoors in controlled growing environments. The estimated production costs in *Table 1* do not include processing costs, which are estimated to add an additional $20 to $35 per pound.

Table 1. Estimated Production Costs of Legalized Marijuana

Production Method	Estimated Cost per Pound
Indoor Production -Five foot by five foot "hobbyist"	$225 + an in-kind compensation for the hobbyist's time
-1,500 square foot residential house	$200 to $400
-One acre 50% covered with greenhouses	$70 to $215
Outdoor Production	
-Commercial-grade, low estimate	$1
-Commercial-grade, mid estimate	$8
-Commercial-grade, high estimate	$10
-High-quality, sinsemilla-equivalent resin	$265

Source: Jonathan P. Caulkins, Estimated Cost of Production for Legalized Cannabis, RAND Corporation, July 2010, at http://www.rand.org/pubs/working_ papers/WR764.html.

Notes: See Caulkins (2010) for details on methodology. Indoor production costs include consumable materials (e.g., soil, water), lighting, labor, and structure/rent. Outdoor production estimates vary based on estimated yield, density of plantings, and labor costs. Calculations assume all output is commercial grade, but the THC-levels across all methods of production are not assumed to be equal. Production costs do not include processing costs, which Caulkins (2010) estimates could add $20 to $35 per pound.

Producing high-quality marijuana in greenhouses appears to cost, at the upper limit, $215 plus $35 per pound for processing, or around $15 per ounce. Using outdoor production, of $10 plus $35 a pound, the cost is about $2.80 per ounce. These products vary by THC concentration; as noted earlier, *sinsemilla* contains 10% -18% THC, or about three times the potency conventional commercial-grade marijuana that is pollinated.

In a different estimate, Easton (2009) indicates that government-sponsored marijuana in Canada can be produced at 33 cents per gram ($9 per ounce or $144 per pound).[48] He also suggests that, based on tobacco sales, the cost per gram of going to a retail market is about 10 cents per gram, or $2.80 per ounce ($44.80 per pound). Adding this amount to estimated costs leads to a cost (and expected price) of $5-$18 per ounce ($80-$288 per pound).

In jurisdictions where marijuana has become quasi-legal, prices tend to be lower than the street price in most cases but higher than these cost estimates. In an article indicating an increased price for medical marijuana in Canada, the price was listed as $1.80-$5 per gram to the final consumer, $50-$140 per ounce. In that same article, a lawyer representing numerous suppliers said his clients could supply for $1-$4 per gram, or $28-$110 per ounce.[49] The street price was listed as $10-$15 per gram, or $280-$420 per ounce. Of course, the price could be discounted if bought in larger quantities. These street prices are high compared with the averages in priceofweed.com. Beginning in April 2014, the Canadian government set the price of medical marijuana at $7.60 (CAD) per gram, which is higher than the current average and closer to the street price.[50] Small growers and homegrown marijuana will no longer be permitted under the new law. These prices are higher than the costs discussed above but also apparently do not reflect an unfettered and mature competitive market.

Actual prices can also be observed in Colorado marijuana shops through online websites, such as Leafly.com. Leafly is a website and mobile phone application that helps users find marijuana shops, medical marijuana dispensaries, and doctors that prescribe medical marijuana located in their areas.[51] Like the consumer website and application, Yelp (which is used to review restaurants, stores, and other sites of interest), Leafly provides consumer reviews of each location and various strands of marijuana and provides “menu” prices of products available at each shop. According to an examination by the authors of some of the most-reviewed marijuana shops in Denver, a gram of marijuana is priced around $9 to $15, an eighth of an ounce of marijuana can be priced around $29 to $40, and an ounce can be priced around $190 to $350.[52] Some of the higher prices listed on Leafly include tax, but it is unclear from the “menu prices” whether some of the prices are before or after tax (although they are most likely before tax, unless noted).

Submissions to priceofweed.com report that marijuana prices in Colorado are lower than the national prices reported earlier, with high quality at $238 per ounce and medium quality at $197 per ounce (compared with $377 and $245 reported for the United States overall). These prices still reflect a mix of the illicit and legal markets but would presumably include taxes on any legal purchases.[53]

Colorado prices provide some indication of falling prices with legalization, but prices appear not close to the cost of production. The prices in Colorado, however, may not reflect those in a fully legal market because they are still in a quasi-legal status. Because the federal government does not recognize the legality of these operations, media reports indicate that these producers may have trouble getting banking assistance, including deposit accounts, much less business loans.[54] These operations are potentially subject to very large federal income taxes, which can be imposed without allowing for deductions because they remain illegal. These taxes can be the equivalent of excise taxes at the federal rate and can apply at each stage of production. (See discussion in *Appendix B*.) And marijuana businesses are still subject to the threat of potential enforcement from federal authorities.

In a 2010 study of the possible effects of legalization in California, researchers from the RAND Corporation estimate that the pretax retail price of marijuana would likely decrease by more than 80%,[55] suggesting a price of $40-$60 per ounce. Miron and Waldock, however, estimate a 50% price reduction, based on a comparison of prices in the United States and the Netherlands (sold in coffee shops).[56] This price reduction would suggest a price of $100-$150 per ounce on average. The Netherlands, however, is, like Colorado, not an instance of a fully legalized market because the Netherlands bans imports and has anti-drug laws on the books.

Although the range of projected prices in a fully legal market is wide, from a few dollars to $100 per ounce, street prices of $200-$300 per ounce suggest that there could be a wide scope for a tax rate designed to align legalized marijuana prices close to current street prices of illegal marijuana. For example, if the eventual competitive price is $50 per ounce and the average street price is $250 per ounce, there is scope for taxes up to $200 tax per ounce.

There are several caveats to this point. The first is state and local governments will likely collect a tax that will absorb some of the differential. The second is a tax that is set too high would encourage the illicit market, and one of the advantages of legalizing marijuana is to largely eliminate the illicit market, reducing law enforcement costs. Moreover, the potential scope of the difference is uncertain, but lowering tax and observing market conditions may be the best initial strategy.

Funding Marijuana Research and Information Programs

Some or all of the yield from a marijuana tax could be used to fund marijuana research. Medical marijuana, as noted, has been approved by 23 states and the District of Columbia. Research on the effects of medical marijuana, which would be helpful in providing guidance to patients and doctors, could be funded in part by the tax.[57] A recent report by the American College of Physicians noted that limitations on marijuana research are caused, in part, by barriers encountered for federal approval, the lack of high-grade, research-quality marijuana, and the general classification of marijuana as a Schedule I illegal drug.[58] The report discusses a wide range of conditions that marijuana may be beneficial for and urges study of the efficacy and side effects of marijuana.

With legalization it would also be more feasible to study a wide array of issues (as discussed in this report), such as externalities, addictive properties, and health effects on recreational as well as medical users. Revenue could also be used to finance information programs on both the risks of marijuana use and to discourage consumption by minors.

Raising Revenue

Historically, the primary purposes of excise taxes in the United States have been to raise revenue, including revenues for emergency spending.[59] Cigarette taxes have been used to offset higher spending levels on health care, such as the Children's Health Insurance Program (CHIP), in recent years.[60]

Given assumptions about price and demand, an excise tax on marijuana can be designed in such a way to achieve a certain revenue target. This section provides some illustrations of how much revenue might be raised from an excise tax were marijuana to become legal. These revenue consequences are quite uncertain given the broad uncertainty about potential price and quantity in the market.

In addition, casual consumers may enter the marijuana market and increase revenue. These consumers may purchase marijuana because concerns about punishment are no longer present or because of a distaste for participating in illegal activities in general. These effects are not necessarily captured in the existing price elasticity estimates (which mostly reflect consumers that are determined enough to defy law enforcement to consume marijuana), and the legal market, even setting price aside, could be much larger than the current market for this reason.

The pace of legalization and taxation of marijuana at the state level could also affect potential revenue collected from a federal excise tax. If more states tend to legalize marijuana, and try to set their excise tax rates to roughly equalize the price of legal (under state laws) marijuana with illicit marijuana, then federal lawmakers could be more constrained in their ability to levy excise taxes on marijuana without encouraging production in the illicit market.[61]

Some analysts have tried to estimate the potential revenue that could be raised from nationwide legalization of marijuana using various economic models, and may in some cases include excise taxes.[62] (Legalization itself would presumably increase revenues by moving more of national income into legal sectors subject to income, such as sales and business taxes, even without an excise tax.)

Miron and Waldock of the Cato Institute estimate that a federal excise tax could raise $5.8 billion (in 2008 dollars) annually in excise taxes if marijuana is taxed at a rate equal to 50% of its price to consumers.[63] Their calculations assume the national market for marijuana at $13.13 billion (in 2008), a 50% fall in price after legalization, and a 25% increase in consumption. They also estimate $3.3 billion in annual savings in expenditures from law enforcement. Miron and Waldock do not report price and quantity separately, but they are probably estimating a tax of around $50-$75 per ounce. Miron and Waldock note that their market size estimates, which are extrapolated from survey data, are small by comparison with other estimates. At the same time, they appear to be assuming a greater response from consumers than that suggested by the literature review.

A Sample Calculation

This calculation outlines how to estimate revenues from an excise tax, using the example of a $50 per ounce tax. It takes into account the effects on aggregate consumption and interactions with income taxes. The results depend on the specific assumptions about market conditions as well as state and proposed federal taxes.

To estimate revenue yield, data on price and quantity are needed. As noted earlier, data on the value of the market ranged from $30 billion to $60 billion according to ONDCP. The current price was estimated at between $200 and $300 per ounce. For this example, assume intermediate values of a $40 billion market and a $250 current price.

To illustrate the potential effect on revenue assume a fully legalized industry nationwide, assume a pretax price of $50 per ounce, a state tax of $50 per ounce, and the consequences of a federal tax of $50 per ounce. The taxes and costs bring the total price to $150 per ounce.

The federal excise tax collection, therefore, is $50 multiplied by the quantity (in ounces). In the current market, quantity would be determined by dividing $40 billion by $250. If quantity did not change the federal excise tax revenue would be \$50 multiplied by \$40 billion divided by \$250, or \$8 billion. Collections, however, would be somewhat larger because the fall in price from legalization would increase consumption. Using a constant elastic formula, the ratio of the new quantity to the old is (P*/P)^E, P* is the new price, P is the old price, and E is the price elasticity (which is negative). Assuming a price elasticity of -0.25, the effect of legalization alone, which is assumed to reduce the price to \$50 per ounce, would lead to a 50% increase in quantity. With federal, state, and local taxes, the price is \$150 and the increase in quantity is 14%, leading to a projected excise tax collection of \$9.1 billion. By comparison, the tax on alcoholic beverages is \$10 billion, a much lower tax applied to a much larger market.[64]

The actual revenue gained is, according to standard estimating conventions, reduced by 25% to account for the loss of income and wage taxes because excise taxes produce a wedge between output and income.[65] Thus the projected revenue gain is \$6.8 billion.[66] As a reminder, this estimate is based on a series of assumptions, changes to which would alter the revenue estimate.

The yield will also depend on how widespread the movement for legalization is and whether medical marijuana is covered. Currently only Colorado and Washington allow recreational marijuana, and they represent less than 4% of the population, so the short-term yield might be less than \$300 million. More revenue would be gained if medical marijuana in other states were taxed.

Using Data from Colorado to Estimate Market Size

As previously mentioned, calculations based on data from the illicit market for marijuana might not be representative of a fully commercialized market. Given the scale of policy changes at the state level, tax collection data from Colorado and Washington could serve as early indicators of the potential tax base of a national legalized market.

Marijuana sales are subject to several layers of taxation at the state and local level. In Colorado, recreational marijuana sales are subject to three different state taxes: (1) a 15% marijuana excise tax on the unprocessed product, (2) a 10% retail marijuana excise tax, and (3) a 2.9% general sales tax. The approximate effective tax rate on marijuana products is between 15% and 25%, before the imposition of the state's 2.9% general sales tax.[67] Medical marijuana in Colorado is subject to the 2.9% general sales tax. Local taxes, such as the Denver city sales tax, can also apply on top of the state taxes.

From January 2014 to September 2014, Colorado has collected more than \$37.0 million in sales taxes, excise taxes, and retail license fees on recreational marijuana (in addition to $13.7 million collected from medical marijuana sales taxes and license fees).[68]

By extrapolating from the actual tax revenue data from Colorado, the national market for marijuana could be estimated. These calculations are detailed in *Appendix C*. After adjusting the September 2014 tax data from Colorado to control for usage rates in different states, it can be estimated that the national sales tax base for recreational marijuana could be between $15.9 billion and $17.0 billion per year (assuming market conditions currently in Colorado prevail nationally).[69] It is difficult to extrapolate medical marijuana data in Colorado to the general U.S. population due to incomplete data in some states, but the tax collections data from Colorado indicate that medical marijuana consumption could roughly double that consumption base.[70]

The combined medical and recreational marijuana sales in Colorado roughly extrapolated to the United States suggest a market of at least $30 billion, which is small compared with most estimates considering that the price should be smaller than in the illicit markets. It may be that the Colorado market is insufficiently developed, and substantial levels of illicit sales are continuing (either due to lower prices on the illicit market or preexisting relationships between buyers and sellers in the black market). However, consumption in Colorado could be overstated due to nonresident sales (also known as "pot tourism").

The estimates do, however, suggest that the issue of whether to exempt medical marijuana and how to enforce any medical exemption that might develop are potentially important issues.

DESIGN ISSUES FOR A FEDERAL MARIJUANA EXCISE TAX

Aside from the general level of the tax, there are a number of design issues for an excise tax discussed in this section.

Choosing the Stage of Production to Levy an Excise Tax

In general, an excise tax that is levied at earlier stages of production has lower administrative costs and fewer opportunities for tax evasion. In most situations, consumers vastly outnumber producers. Trying to implement an excise tax at the consumer retail outlet often results in a duplication of processes and increases the risk of tax evasion.[71] As a result, federal excise taxes are generally levied on manufacturers and imports (with an exemption for exports).

Choosing the Excise Tax Base

In general, marijuana can be taxed based on a per unit measurement or the product price. Each tax base has its own advantages and disadvantages, and multiple tax bases could be combined.

Weight

A tax by weight is similar to the federal excise tax regime for tobacco because regulations limit the per unit size of cigarettes, cigars, etc. A tax by weight is relatively easy to administer (after accounting for moisture content). The tax could be levied based on the "wet" weight, right after the leaves and flowers are picked, or the weight after drying.[72] A weight-based tax would need to be administered at the manufacturing level, as a retail-based weight tax could create significant issues for different types of products.[73] However, a weight-based tax could encourage the production of more potent marijuana.

Potency

Most potency-based tax proposals are based on the per-ounce THC content. In comparison to a weight-based tax, a potency-based tax could be more complicated and costly to enforce and administer. The largest administrative hurdle to a potency-based tax is ensuring that lab testing of marijuana strains is accurate and reliable. Regulations defining the number and weight of any samples that producers need to submit for testing would be required. According to one lab in Oakland, CA, samples of two grams can be used to evaluate the potency of up to two pounds of marijuana. Costs of these lab tests can be much as $100-$120 per sample, and as low as $60-$75 per test with a bulk discount. If marijuana is legalized, it can be expected that more labs that perform similar services will enter the market, and possibly reduce the price of testing. More competition in testing could encourage the development of more reliable technology, but it could also lead growers to pick a lab that tends to understate the amount of THC in a product.[74]

Ultimately, it could be difficult to measure final THC content with any degree of reliability, given the nature of some marijuana products. Another disadvantage to a tax based on THC potency is that it could encourage more consumption of less-potent marijuana. If the public health costs of smoking marijuana outweigh the health costs of consuming more potent marijuana, then the effects of this option might be undesirable.[75]

An alternative potency calculation could be based on the ratio of THC to cannabidiol (CBD). Such a tax base could encourage consumers to purchase marijuana with more sedative effects.

Price

A tax could be levied as a percentage (ad valorem) of the manufacturers or retail sales price of marijuana. Ad valorem taxes have several advantages: they (1) automatically adjust for changes in price, and (2) can be easily applied to a wide variety of products that might otherwise be difficult to quantify in a per unit manner. Both the tax regimes in Colorado and Washington use some form of an ad valorem tax on wholesalers as one method to tax marijuana, and H.R. 501, the Marijuana Tax Equity Act of 2013, proposes a 50% tax on the producer or importer price. The main disadvantage of an ad valorem tax is the required regulations to specify the taxable price the taxes apply to.

A manufacturers tax (i.e., imposed after the plant is first grown and harvested) is the most simple form of administration because there are generally fewer firms involved in manufacturing than retailing. Most federal excise taxes are imposed at the manufacturer stage (e.g., tobacco, alcohol, firearms). For vertically integrated firms that are both manufacturers and retailers (or some other sort of intermediate firm, such as a wholesaler), regulations need to identify how to construct a manufacturers price if no market transaction takes place.

In contrast, a retail tax regime, resembling a sales tax, could be created to capture any price markup due to the type of product or any "market power" of firms with branding or advertising advantages. The price of a product containing marijuana or THC could be determined by a number of characteristics other than its intoxication potential.[76]

Special Considerations

In the case of a per unit tax (e.g., weight or potency), the tax rate can be indexed for inflation using some sort of measure of price changes, such as increases in the Consumer Price Index (CPI). Most other federal excise taxes are unindexed (e.g., alcohol, tobacco, gasoline), and, as a result, have declined in real value over time, absent legislative increases in statutory tax rates.[77]

Given the uncertainty over prices and demand after legalization, sunset provisions for the tax could be incorporated into any initial authorizing language of a marijuana tax. Sunset provisions could encourage legislators to revisit marijuana tax laws to better reflect the evolving conditions of the nascent, legalized industry. For example, the initial tax rate for legalized marijuana could be set low enough to undermine the illicit market, but then increased gradually to set the tax rate high enough to limit consumption. Alternatively, legislation could delegate authority to the Secretary of the Treasury (or a similar official) to adjust tax rates according to certain criteria.

Other Options

Various methods of taxation could also be combined. For example, a general tax on marijuana could be levied based on price or weight, with either a surcharge for higher-THC products or differential rates for various products, such as edibles. Differential tax rates could help shape consumption in such a way that it could reduce some of the negative social costs of marijuana. But, different tax rates could add complexity and unequal tax burdens across various marijuana consumers.

By comparison, alcohol is taxed by potency (i.e., alcohol content) as well as category, with taxes per alcohol content lower for beer and wine than for distilled spirits. Cigarettes are taxed on a per unit basis. Cigars are subject to an ad valorem tax with a high ceiling, although the tax is imposed at the manufacturers' level.

Tax Treatment of Existing Plant and Product Inventories

The initiation of a federal marijuana tax could also raise the question of whether to integrate existing stocks of marijuana into the tax base.[78] Lawmakers would have to address the taxation of marijuana plants and any consumer goods sold in jurisdictions that have legalized medical and recreational sales. Integrating more preexisting marijuana plants and products into the tax base could enable producers and retailers to better meet the initial demand for marijuana (at prices potentially low enough to undercut the illegal market), reduce complexity between federal and local tax regulations, and increase initial federal tax revenue. However, some preexisting marijuana plants and products might not comply with new federal regulations or purity standards that are likely to accompany any federal tax regime.

An alternative option could include ample lead time between the enactment of such a tax and the effective date of the first legalized sales, giving producers sufficient time to comply with any federal regulations. Although this might help legal producers and retailers compete with the underground market, it would add complexity to the multiple layers of taxation of marijuana in some jurisdictions.

Colorado and Washington have taken slightly different approaches to this issue. In Colorado, retail licenses were initially issued to existing medical marijuana dispensaries (some of which were already growing their own plants).[79] In Washington, current plants grown indoors or outdoors can be converted to legal stocks if the owner has a producer license and the growing space meets all of the state's guidelines.[80]

In general, when federal excise taxes are increased, untaxed floor stocks are subject to tax (sometimes with exemptions for small retail operations). The purpose is to prevent building up inventories in advance of the effective date of the tax.

Restrictions, Exemptions, and Special Tax Treatment

Several issues could arise concerning restrictions, exemptions, and special treatment under a federal tax on marijuana. Policy makers could choose to implement such regulations at the federal level or allow the states to make their own laws pertaining to each of these issues. Any of these differential tax treatments, however, would make the tax more complicated.

Age Restrictions

State laws in Colorado and Washington limit recreational marijuana purchases to individuals aged 21 or older. Age restrictions could have a limiting effect on the tax base, as surveys indicate that younger individuals use marijuana at higher rates than those over 26 years old.[81] However, this trend could change post-legalization as the stigma among adult use lessens and the exotic appeal of an illicit drug lessens among youth. In any case, excluding these consumers from the legal tax base could support some underground production activity (which would be untaxed), or indirect sales of legally purchased marijuana through of-age connections (which could still be preferable to direct transactions with illicit dealers).

Customer Purchasing or Possession Limits

Under state law, Colorado residents are allowed to possess up to one ounce of marijuana and make as many transactions as desired as long as they do not exceed the one ounce limit. Non-Colorado residents are restricted to purchasing one quarter of an ounce (7 grams) in a single transaction. The restriction on non-residents is primarily intended to reduce the risks for larger-scale diversion or export. It has yet to be seen if this restriction has had a significant effect on diversion. More restrictive purchasing limits (by weight) coupled with an ad valorem tax rate can also serve to increase the effective tax rate on heavy users, who are more likely to benefit from a bulk discount.

Production Limits

Production limits could be enacted based on the total market size or per grower. Washington has a target of 80 metric tons (half for dried marijuana and half for marijuana-extract based products, such as edibles and lotions) for the maximum size of its marijuana market. The primary rationales behind this policy are to monitor possible diversion of sales to other states and guide the number of licenses issued.[82] Colorado has no target. Similarly, concerns could be raised about the diversion of underground exports from the United States to countries where marijuana is still illegal. A tax administered closer to the beginning of the production chain might be more capable of monitoring such diversion. Mark Kleiman, Professor of Public Policy at UCLA and former marijuana policy consultant to the state of Washington, has been quoted as saying that a production limit could also reduce the power of larger producers who, if left unregulated, could increase the negative social consequences of marijuana consumption in pursuit of maximizing profit.[83]

In general, production limits generate inefficiency and can contribute to windfall profits for firms already in the market. Production limits have never been considered for any other commodity by the federal government and are unlikely to work for states and a national legal market.

Exemption or Inclusion of Medical Marijuana

The tax treatment of medical marijuana varies in the jurisdictions that have legalized medical marijuana. Each jurisdiction applies its general sales tax or a special gross receipts or revenue tax on medical marijuana. For example, medical marijuana sold in Colorado is subject to the 2.9% general, state sales tax but is not subject to the 10% retail marijuana state sales tax or the 15% retail marijuana excise tax.

Medical marijuana, and the extent to which users are in medical need, is an issue that is contentious. This use might be more attractive to consumers who hesitate or dislike participating in an illicit market. Evidence suggests a negative correlation between medical marijuana and prescription drugs because deaths from prescription drug overdoses have declined in states with medical marijuana.[84]

Although there is a possible justification for exempting this medical use, differences in the after-tax price of recreational and medical marijuana could also provide incentives for users to seek out medical prescriptions. As indicated by the analysis of tax data in Colorado, exempting medical marijuana from a federal tax could also significantly limit the tax base if strict standards for medical prescriptions are not enforced. Preventing such abuse, however, could significantly increase the cost of tax administration.

If medical marijuana is exempt, and the tax is imposed at the production level, producers would have to know the end use of the product. Thus, a segregation of sales of medical marijuana and a marking or stamping device would likely be necessary.

Exemption for Home Production

Rules vary across different products that are subject to excise taxation.[85] Colorado allows individuals to grow up to six plants for recreational use, and households can grow up to 12 plants. Washington does not allow home growing of marijuana for recreational use.[86] In comparison, in federal law, no home distilling of alcohol is legal, whereas wine and beer can be made in limited amounts, and tobacco can be grown without limit.

If home production is allowed and exempt from taxation, another issue is whether a quantity limit should apply and if so what that limit might be. Pat Oglesby, former chief tax counsel of the Senate Finance Committee and noted expert on state marijuana taxes, indicates that a single plant can yield 448 grams (or approximately a pound of marijuana) and the average user consumes about 100 grams (less than four ounces) per year, so any home-growing limit would probably be seen as high.[87] At the same time, Oglesby (2011) argues that production for home use is not likely to be much of a threat to the tax because even with high illicit prices, even where homegrown is legal, users participated in the illicit market rather than growing their own. However, Caulkins et al., suggest that home production would seriously undermine enforcement because anyone in possession of nontaxed product could claim home production.[88] Banning home production could also increase the revenue generated from a marijuana tax.

Special Tax Rates for Small Producers

Small wine and beer producers are eligible for lower tax rates, so there is some precedent for tax reductions for small producers. This exemption or lower rate would be linked to a point of collection at the packaging and distribution level. The value of a lower tax for small producers is not clear. In general, however, it is more efficient to collect the tax from a few larger producers, and a benefit for small firms would act against that objective.

Additionally, a small businesses exemption could encourage larger forms of evasion, because processing and distribution may be easier on a small scale.

Special Tax Rates for More Energy Efficient Production

Another possibility is to apply a lower tax to marijuana grown outdoors, which uses less energy than indoor growing. One study indicates that legalization could reduce the price of marijuana, and lead to less costly cultivation practices outdoors rather than indoors.[89] In contrast, concerns exist that outdoor marijuana cultivation could divert land and bodies of water, thereby generating another set of negative environmental effects.[90] Incentives to produce higher-potency marijuana (e.g., a tax rate based on weight) could encourage indoor production, where growing conditions can be better managed.

Occupational Taxes

Another federal tax option is levying a special occupational tax (SOT) on any business involved in the production, distribution, or sales of marijuana. SOTs are not licensing fees. Generally, SOTs are levied as a flat fee annually on each firm and comprise a small amount of revenue relative to excise taxes. Currently, federal SOTs are collected on certain businesses in the tobacco or firearms industry. Segments of the alcohol trade were also subject to SOTs until they were repealed in 2008.[91]

The Marijuana Tax Equity Act of 2013 (H.R. 501) would impose an occupational tax of $1,000 per year on each marijuana producer, importer, or manufacturer, and a $500 per year tax for any other person engaged in a marijuana enterprise.

TAX ADMINISTRATION, ENFORCEMENT, AND OTHER REGULATIONS

History suggests that the role of enforcement and administrative efforts could be the difference between a sustainable and unsustainable federal tax regime on marijuana. The illicit trade and importation of bootleg spirits in the United States continued after Prohibition ended in 1934 until cuts in tariff rates on spirit imports were negotiated with trading partners (thereby lowering the price of legal spirits), and until the Department of the Treasury hired or assigned more than 1,000 agents to work on enforcing alcohol-related laws during the late 1930s.[92]

Today, marijuana enforcement efforts would have to deter regular consumers from engaging in illicit transactions with dealers they have presumably built a relationship of trust with in terms of secrecy and product integrity. Additionally, enforcement would have to compel producers to obtain licenses and pay taxes. Without increasing resources for tax-enforcement authorities commensurate with federal-policy change, legalizing and taxing marijuana would likely undermine the long-term viability of any federal tax base.

Tracking the Production of Legal Marijuana

Some tax experts have noted that marijuana smuggling might be more prevalent compared with illegal alcohol production because marijuana is more compact and easier to transport than alcohol.[93] However, marijuana is more pungent than packaged alcohol.

Collecting a tax closer to the point of production, rather than point of sales, could reduce the number of taxable entities and increase the scale of tax units that would need to be monitored (e.g., greenhouses compared to joints). If the tax is applied early in the stage of production, some marker or evidence that the tax has been paid would be needed. As with the case of alcohol and tobacco, tax stamps could be used, or seals on packages (although packages can be opened and refilled, so this method is not completely foolproof). If sold as joints, individual marks could be put on each paper cylinder. Another possibility is the use of dye. New technological developments are also discussed by Oglesby, such as genetic markers or tracking systems that would monitor production from seed to final sale.[94]

Colorado developed several planks for its enforcement system. It tracks marijuana plants from "seed to sale" using radio frequency identification (RFID) tags attached to each plant.[95] When the plant is harvested, the leaves and buds are given a new RFID tag and a label printed with the plant's authorized source.[96] Marijuana enterprises are required to report their inventory to the Colorado Department of Revenue's Marijuana Enforcement Division through a linked-computer system called Marijuana Inventory Tracking Solutions (MITS). These systems are meant to complement traditional forms of enforcement, such as physical surveillance.

Labeling and Measurement

Regulations that would standardize weights and potency measurements would most likely need to accompany a marijuana tax regime. Such a regime would contribute to consumer safety and more accurate dosing. Additionally, the U.S. Department of the Treasury could develop marketing standards on the issues related to labeling and branding of different strains of marijuana.[97] These marketing standards are currently negotiated with industry representatives as a means to inform consumers and prevent competition from domestic and imported products that do not meet the same standards. For example, regulations could define what can be labeled "indica," "sativa," or certain types of hybrid strands.

Strict Enforcement of Medical Marijuana Prescription Standards

As previously mentioned, different tax rates in medical and recreational marijuana could create significant arbitrage opportunities for consumers. This is particularly the case for heavy users, who stand the most to gain from evading a significant excise tax burden.[98] Medical marijuana dispensaries are typically organized as nonprofit organizations. Thus, enforcement of regulations will also be important for proper collection of income taxes if these nonprofits are allowed to organize as Section 501(c) entities.

Distinguishing Marijuana from Industrial Hemp

Hemp has no commercial value as a psychoactive due to its low concentrations of THC. The 113th Congress made changes to U.S. policies regarding industrial hemp during the omnibus farm bill debate. The Agricultural Act of 2014 (H.R. 2642; commonly known as the "farm bill") includes a provision that would allow certain research institutions and also state departments of agriculture to grow industrial hemp, if allowed under state laws where the institution or state department of agriculture is located.[99] Because hemp is a useful agricultural plant, some might also think that it would be reasonable to legalize hemp for industrial production (and exempt it from taxation) if marijuana is legalized for commercial production.

For tax purposes, hemp could be distinguished from marijuana for purposes of taxes by its THC quantity. Oglesby notes that proposed legislation in the United States used a THC content of less than 1/2 of 1% and less than 1% by weight to distinguish hemp from marijuana. Europe and Canada currently allow hemp to be grown and require less than 0.3% THC by weight to distinguish legal hemp from illegal marijuana.

An argument made by Oglesby (and others) is that marijuana can be hidden in hemp fields, one reason that hemp is illegal. This claim is likely overstated, as cross-pollination would weaken the effectiveness of the marijuana plants.[100]

As previously mentioned, higher-quality strains of marijuana require controlled climates isolated from pollination in order to reach peak THC potency.

Effects of Federal Marijuana Laws on State Tax and Regulatory Regimes

Some experts have also noted that the decision, or delay, of legalization at the federal level could have significant effects on the development of marijuana tax policy at the state level. As long as marijuana remains illegal at the federal level, states with marijuana legalization laws could rely on a system of licensing private businesses to grow and sell marijuana, instead of systems in which a state-based monopoly regulates the sale of marijuana (i.e., as some states currently have over liquor retail sales).[101] Proponents of state-based monopolies see them as a tool to regulate consumption (e.g., state-approved retail locations, restricted marketing), while opponents of state-based monopolies see them as susceptible to corruption, and driven mostly for purposes of raising revenue (a common critique of many state-run lottery commissions).[102]

Although the differences in the level of revenue extracted from a licensing scheme versus a state monopoly scheme might be difficult to predict or even negligible, the dominance of licensing systems across states could make it difficult for lawmakers to roll back such systems and encourage state monopolies (for whatever reasons) in the future.[103]

Conclusion

The uncertainty over many aspects of marijuana creates difficulties in arriving at conclusions about the possible effects of a legalized and taxed marijuana market.

These uncertainties include the post-legalization price of marijuana (and even the current illicit price), the size of the market, and the response of consumers to price changes. These aspects make the projection of revenues for a particular tax uncertain. The uncertainty about prices as well as the spillover and health effects of marijuana makes the setting of the level of the tax difficult. Even choosing how to impose the tax is limited by uncertainties as to differential consumer response to potency and price and the compliance costs of taxing for potency.

In terms of revenue-raising potential, it appears that the tax base for legalized marijuana sales is much more limited compared with alcohol or tobacco, at least in the short term. This outcome is particularly the case if medical marijuana sales are exempt from a federal marijuana tax.

Appendix A. Some Additional Social Costs and Benefits of Marijuana

The discussion in the text reported some broader information on the magnitude of the social costs and benefits of marijuana. This appendix discusses some of the components of those social costs.

Relationship between Marijuana and Alcohol Consumption

One of the potential determinants of social costs of marijuana legalization is the relationship between marijuana consumption and alcohol consumption. Social costs of alcohol consumption have been well documented in academic studies.[104] If marijuana is a *substitute* for alcohol, then arguably marijuana has some positive spillover effects on society because marijuana consumption has fewer social costs than alcohol consumption.[105] However, if marijuana is consumed with alcohol, then arguably marijuana results in some negative spillover effects on society.

Researchers have not reached a consensus on this issue.[106] Many economic studies that measure the relationship between marijuana and other substances (i.e., cross-price elasticity of demand) do not capture long-term effects, could be measuring spurious relationships, or examine individuals who might not be representative of the national population.[107] Marijuana research is highly regulated in the United States. The National Institute on Drug Abuse, the agency primarily responsible for policy research, has been quoted in media sources that it "does not fund research focused on the potential beneficial medical effects of marijuana."[108] Additionally, no study captures the effects of commercial and recreational legalization on the scale of Colorado or Washington because no other jurisdiction in the world has pursued such policies.

This uncertainty surrounding the relationship between alcohol and marijuana use is important because it limits the plausibility that a marijuana tax could be initially levied based on the external costs to society. For example, marijuana legalization could impose significant external costs or savings on society, even if marijuana consumption has a minor effect on the demand for alcohol due to the relatively large external costs of alcohol consumption.109 Initiatives at the state levels in Colorado and Washington could provide researchers with an opportunity to better understand the effects of broader legalization policies.

Polydrug Use

In addition, the social costs of marijuana legalization could vary based on the relationship between the consumption of marijuana and other illicit drugs (commonly referred to as "polydrug use"). Studies indicate that marijuana has a lower risk of addiction and abuse than cocaine, crack, or heroin.[110] Some claim that marijuana is a "gateway drug" to further illicit drug use. In survey data, about 10% of infrequent marijuana users in the past year report using other illegal drugs whereas the rate for "heavy" marijuana users (21-30 days per month) is slightly more than 25%.[111]

Driving under the Influence

Current research on the effects of marijuana use on traffic fatalities is limited by methodological and technological shortcomings. As noted earlier, some researchers have used controlled experiments to measure the effects of marijuana use on standard driving measurements, such as ability to track driving lanes.[112] Other researchers have studied the extent to which marijuana use has been linked to actual driving fatalities. Among non-alcohol drugs, marijuana is the most frequently detected substance in the general driver population as well as in drivers being involved in crashes.[113] However, this is not the same as saying that there is a causal link between marijuana use and traffic fatalities. Studies using data from actual crash sites typically measure the driver's blood, urine, or saliva for alcohol and metabolites released by the body in reaction to consumption of various types of drugs (including marijuana). Marijuana testing technology is currently limited in its ability to detect the level of marijuana intoxication at a given time. In the words of one study, "it is possible for a driver to test positive for cannabinol in the blood up to one week after use. Thus, the prevalence of nonalcoholic drugs ... should be interpreted as an indicator of use, not necessarily a measure of drug impairment."[114] For example, more advanced metabolite tests or mouth swabs would need to be developed to distinguish between a positive driving under the influence (DUI) test of a recent user and a chronic medical marijuana patient that has not been under the psychoactive effects of marijuana.

Criminal Incarcerations

Some claim that marijuana legalization could lead to savings in criminal justice spending at the federal, state, and local levels. Some of the estimates cited in media sources have been quite large. For example, Jeffrey Miron, a researcher at Harvard University, estimated in 2005 that legalizing marijuana would save $7.7 billion per year in total enforcement costs at state and federal levels.[115]

However, subsequent research suggests that estimates could be much smaller.[116] Sevigny and Caulkins (2004) estimated that 8% of state and federal prison inmates serving sentences for drug law violations were marijuana-only offenders.[117] Some prisoners caught trafficking other drugs could have also possessed marijuana, but these individuals would have been incarcerated even if marijuana were legal.

According to the U.S. Sentencing Commission, 31.2% of offenders in FY2013 were sentenced to a federal prison for a primary offense related to drugs.[118] The vast majority of these sentences are for drug trafficking.[119] Of these drug-related offenses, 28.4% of the sentences were related to marijuana (the highest share among drug-related categories).[120] Federal legalization of marijuana would likely not affect federal inmates already serving sentences for marijuana-related charges. It is unclear how federal legalization of marijuana might impact the future federal prison population.[121]

In state and local jails, drug violations account for about one-fifth of incarcerations and marijuana-only violations account for less than 10% of those charges.[122] According to these estimates, legalizing marijuana could lead to 2% fewer prisoners in jails over time. Federal legalization would likely not affect state and local inmates already serving sentences for marijuana-related charges, and would not affect future state and local incarcerations in jurisdictions that do not choose to legalize it.

These benefits, large or small, would be related to legalizing marijuana, not taxing it. If taxes or regulations are so large or onerous that they encourage a continuation of the illicit market, some of these gains would be lost.

Marijuana-Related Crime, Violence, and Corruption

The majority of costs associated with the black market for illicit drugs are related to illegal stimulants and opiates, not marijuana. This is because the price per pound of these other drugs is typically more than marijuana. Many marijuana exchanges take place indoors among parties (such as friends and family) where there is less risk for conflict, whereas many other drug transactions take place outdoors among strangers or in public.[123]

APPENDIX B. CURRENT TREATMENT OF THE DEDUCTIBILITY OF EXPENSES FOR MARIJUANA-RELATED BUSINESSES

Marijuana producers and retailers may not deduct the costs of selling their product (e.g., payroll, rent, and advertising) for the purposes of the federal tax filings.[124] The Internal Revenue Code (IRC) Section 280E states that

> No deduction or credit shall be allowed for any amount paid or incurred during the taxable year in carrying on any trade or business if such trade or business (or the activities which comprise such trade or business) consists of trafficking in controlled substances (within the meaning of schedule I and II of the Controlled Substances Act) which is prohibited by Federal law or the law of any State in which such trade or business is conducted.

Media reports indicate that the Internal Revenue Service (IRS) has enforced this provision in audits of marijuana-related businesses by refusing to accept these business deductions.[125] Effectively this constitutes an implicit tax on marijuana-related businesses equal to the value of the tax benefit of such deductions if firms engaged in an industry that was legal under federal law.

Some businesses have challenged the IRS's practices through the courts. For example, Sacramento-based, Canna Care marijuana dispensary is challenging IRS tax penalties of more than $800,000 in a case before the U.S. tax court in San Francisco, CA. Media reports indicate that the IRS refused to accept $2.6 million in business deductions for employee salaries, rent, and other costs over three years (although the IRS allowed Canna Care to deduct the cost of the marijuana itself).[126]

The discrepancies between federal and state and local tax treatments of marijuana-related businesses create economic incentives to engage in the underground economy. In addition to the uncertainty of federal tax enforcement procedures (and costs of any related legal assistance), the inability of marijuana businesses to deduct their business expenses is effectively an implicit tax up to 39.6% (if organized as sole-proprietor or partnership) or 35% (if organized as a corporation) of the cost of these expenses.[127] These implicit taxes are paid in addition to state and local sales and special excise taxes.[128]

The status quo administration of federal tax laws creates an economic advantage for illicit marijuana sellers, who are not subject to direct taxation of their sales.

In the 113th Congress, the Small Business Tax Equity Act of 2013 (H.R. 2240) would exempt a business that conducts marijuana sales in compliance with state law from the IRC Section 280E prohibition against allowing business-related tax credits or deductions for expenditures in connection with trafficking in controlled substances.

APPENDIX C. TECHNICAL CALCULATIONS FOR THE ESTIMATE OF A NATIONAL MARIJUANA TAX BASE FROM COLORADO DATA

An estimate of the total sales volume of a national sales base can be calculated by extrapolating tax collection data from Colorado or Washington. Data from both states likely underrepresent total demand because licenses for more production and retail businesses are pending. Additionally, it is unknown if the underground market for marijuana significantly declined from the opening of state-licensed stores.

For the purposes of this report, the most recent tax revenue data from Colorado are used to calculate an estimate of the state's marijuana tax base (dollar amount of total sales). The recreational tax base can be calculated using tax collections data from the 10% retail marijuana sales tax or the 2.9% general sales tax (which provide two measures to derive the total tax base), where tax base is equal to tax collections divided by the tax rate.[129] Because each of the two taxes yields slightly different tax bases, the two calculations are averaged to determine a monthly aggregate tax base for recreational sales.

For example, the Colorado Department of Revenue reported that the 10% retail marijuana sales tax collected $2.9 million[130] and the 2.9% sales tax collected $886,915 (on retail, non-medical marijuana) in September 2014.[131] Using the methodology above, this would lead to tax base calculations of $29.4 million and $30.6 million, respectively.[132] Averaging these two numbers leads to an estimate of $30.0 million in recreational marijuana sales in the state of Colorado in September 2014. 133

The data from Colorado can then be extrapolated for each state and the District of Columbia to calculate an estimate of the national sales tax base. The recreational sales tax base averaged from the two data points in Colorado can be multiplied by each state's or district's population (indexed, relative to Colorado) and then multiplied by the marijuana usage rates (indexed, relative to Colorado) as reported by the National Survey of Drug Use and Health (NSDUH). In other words, this simple calculation assumes the primary sources of variation in consumption in each state or district are based on population and usage rates and does not assume major changes in price (e.g., the large-scale production of relatively cheap, unbranded marijuana; or variations in state tax rates) that could lead to further supply and demand effects. Using the August 2014 data from Colorado, it can be estimated that the national sales tax base for recreational marijuana could be $14.5 billion or $15.4 billion per year.[134] These estimates could be subject to revision, as recreational tax revenue in Colorado has been generally increasing since January 2014.

A similar process can be used to calculate the medical marijuana tax base in Colorado, although there is only one tax levied on medical marijuana in Colorado (the 2.9% general sales tax). Based on September 2014 data, medical marijuana sales in Colorado were $31.3 million.[135] From January to September 2014, monthly medical marijuana sales in Colorado have ranged between approximately $31 million and $35 million. In FY2013 (ending June 30, 2013), before the legalization of recreational marijuana, state sales tax collections data from the Colorado Department of Revenue imply an annual medical marijuana tax base of $314.2 million in sales.[136] It is too early to conclude whether the opening of the recreational marijuana market has affected the demand for medical marijuana in Colorado.

However, it is difficult to extrapolate medical marijuana data in Colorado to the general U.S. population because of incomplete data in some states.[137] Additionally, the medical marijuana patient data could have a self-selection bias, as some individuals could have been willing to relocate to states permitting medical marijuana use, if they felt that they had few other options to alleviate their condition. Based on Colorado's tax collections data, medical marijuana consumption could double marijuana consumption total amounts, if not more. Even if medical marijuana regulations were more tightly enforced, post-legalization, users denied for a medical card could purchase marijuana for recreational purposes.

End Notes

[1] For a list of jurisdictions that have legalized medical marijuana, see National Conference on State Legislatures, "State Medical Marijuana Laws," at http://www.ncsl.org/research/health/state-medical-marijuana-laws.aspx. For a list of jurisdictions that have decriminalized marijuana possession for personal consumption, see National Organization for the Reform of Marijuana Laws (NORML), "States that Have Decriminalized," at http://norml.org/aboutmarijuana/item/states-that-have-decriminalized.

[2] For a summary of the marijuana-related ballot initiatives approved on November 4, 2014, see Paul Armentano, "State, Local Marijuana Legalization Measures Win Big On Election Day," November 5, 2014, at http://blog.norml.org/2014/11/05/state-local-marijuana-legalization-measures-win-big-on-election-day/.

[3] Under the District of Columbia Home Rule Act of 1973 (P.L. 93-198), DC officials must transmit the legalization bill to Congress. Then, Congress has 60 legislative days to review certain changes to DC's criminal code and 30 legislative days to review other legislative measures. See Council of the District of Columbia, "How a Bill Becomes a Law," at http://dccouncil.us/pages/how-a-bill-becomes-a-law.

[4] See "56% Favor Legalizing, Regulating Marijuana," *Rasmussen Reports*, May 17, 2012, at http://www.rasmussenreports.com/public_content/lifestyle/general_lifestyle/may_2012/56_favor_legalizing_regulating_marijuana; Pew Research Center for the People and the Press, *Majority Now Supports Legalizing Marijuana*, April 4, 2013, at http://www.people-press.org/2013/04/04/majority-now-supports-legalizingmarijuana/; and Art Swift, *For First Time, Americans Favor Legalizing Marijuana*, Gallup, October 22, 2013, at http://www.gallup.com/poll/165539/first-time-americans-favor-legalizing-marijuana.aspx. According to the polls, disagreements exist along ideological lines though, with a majority of Democrats and Independents in favor of legalization but a majority of Republicans are against legalization. A majority of poll respondents, regardless of ideology, agree that government efforts to enforce marijuana laws cost more than they are worth. See Pew Research Center, *Partisans Disagree on Legalization of Marijuana, but Agree on Law Enforcement Policies*, April 30, 2013, at http://www.pewresearch.org/daily-

number/partisans-disagree-on-legalization-of-marijuana-but-agree-on-lawenforcement-policies/. For analysis on select public opinion polls on marijuana, see E.J. Dionne, Jr. and William Galston, *The New Politics of Marijuana Legalization:*, The Brookings Institution, May 2013, at http://www.brookings.edu/research/interactives/2013/politics-of-marijuana-legalization.

[5] These bills are, respectively, the Ending Federal Marijuana Prohibition Act of 2013 (H.R. 499) and the Marijuana Tax Equity Act of 2013 (H.R. 501). Specifically, H.R. 501 would impose a 50% tax on the price sold.

[6] See the National Commission on Federal Marijuana Policy Act of 2013 (H.R. 1635).

[7] The current federal tax treatment of marijuana (as a Schedule I drug) is detailed in *Appendix B.*

[8] This report also assumes some familiarity with the general principles and analysis of excise taxes. For an introduction to excise tax issues, see CRS Report R43189, *Federal Excise Taxes: An Introduction and General Analysis* , by Sean Lowry. Also, it does not consider legal or regulatory issues, except as they relate to excise tax issues. For further information on these issues, see CRS Report R43034, *State Legalization of Recreational Marijuana: Selected Legal Issues*, by Todd Garvey and Brian T. Yeh; CRS Report R43435, *Marijuana: Medical and Retail—Selected Legal Issues*, by Todd Garvey and Charles Doyle; and Rosalie Liccardo Pacula et al., "Developing Public Health Regulations for Marijuana: Lessons From Alcohol and Tobacco," *American Journal of Public Health*, April 17, 2014.

[9] The two major strains of cannabis are indica and sativa; some plants are hybrids. Industrial hemp is a different variety of Cannabis sativa and is the same plant species of marijuana. However, hemp is genetically different and is distinguished by its use and chemical makeup (e.g., containing a THC concentration level of less than 1%), as well as by different cultivation practices in its production. For more information on industrial hemp, see CRS Report RL32725, *Hemp as an Agricultural Commodity*, by Renée Johnson.

[10] For lists of common cannabinoids and their claimed effects, see SC Labs, "Cannabinoids," at http://sclabs.com/learn/learn-cannabinoids.html; CannLabs, "Cannabinoids," at http://www.cannlabs.com/the-science/cannabinoids/; or Steep Hill Labs, "Cannabinoid and Terpenoid Reference Guide," at http://steephilllab.com/resources/cannabinoid-and-terpenoid-reference-guide/.

[11] Jonathan Caulkins et al., *Marijuana Legalization: What Everyone Needs to Know* (Oxford: Oxford UP, 2012), p. 8.

[12] Ibid., p. 22.

[13] Ibid., p. 8.

[14] For definitions of terms relating to marijuana, see Leafly Glossary of Cannabis Terms, at http://www.leafly.com/ knowledge-center/cannabis-101/glossary-of-cannabis-terms; and "Marijuana 101 – The Ultimate Weed Glossary" at http://www.marijuana.com/news /2012/05/marijuana-101-the-ultimate-weed-glossary/.

[15] The external cost cannot account for these taxes, however. Tobacco taxes appear to be imposed at rates well above their external costs to society, whereas alcohol taxes are imposed well below their external costs. After increasing an estimate from a 1994 study by inflation, the external cost per pack of cigarettes is estimated to be around $0.42. See CRS Report 94-214, *Cigarette Taxes to Fund Health Care Reform: An Economic Analysis*, by Jane G. Gravelle and Dennis Zimmerman. After the latest increase in federal cigarette taxes to $1.01 a pack in 2009, the total taxes were estimated at $2.32 (including state and local taxes and the tobacco settlement, which functions as an excise tax). See CRS Report RS22681, *The Cigarette Tax Increase to Finance SCHIP*, by Jane G. Gravelle. The external cost of alcohol is estimated at 97 cents per ounce, compared with combined federal and state taxes of 26

cents per ounce. See CRS Report R43350, *Alcohol Excise Taxes: Current Law and Economic Analysis*, by Sean Lowry.

[16] For example, one study of alcohol places the total costs of U.S. alcohol consumption (additional health costs, loss of productivity, and other costs such as criminal justice) at $223 billion annually. The study identifies 58.5% of those costs as falling on others, which indicates that these costs are $130 billion. Ellen E. Bouchery et al., "Economic Costs of Excessive Alcohol Consumption in the U.S., 2006," *American Journal of Preventive Medicine*, vol. 41, no. 5, November 2011, pp. 516-524, at http://www.ajpmonline.org/article/S0749-3797(11)00538-1/pdf. As noted in the text, estimates adjusting for lifetime costs are $30 billion.

[17] Willard G. Manning et al., *The Costs of Poor Health Habits* (Cambridge, MA: Harvard University Press, 1991).

[18] These calculations are based on data on external cost per ounce compared with tax collection per ounce and tax revenues. See CRS Report R43350, *Alcohol Excise Taxes: Current Law and Economic Analysis*, by Sean Lowry.

[19] David J. Nutt, Leslie A. King, and Lawrence D. Phillips (on Behalf of the Independent Scientific Committee on Drugs), "Drug harms in the UK: a Multicriteria Decision Analysis," *Lancet*, November 2010, vol. 376, pp. 1558-1565.

[20] Gerald Thomas, and Christopher G. Davis, "Cannabis, Tobacco and Alcohol Use in Canada: Comparing risks of Harm and Costs to Society," Reprinted from "Cannabis" issue of *Visions Journal*, 2009, 5 (4), p. 11, at http://www.heretohelp.bc.ca/visions/cannabis-vol5/cannabis-tobacco-and-alcohol-use-in-canada and Comparing the Perceived Seriousness and Actual Costs of Substance Abuse in Canada, Canadian Centre on Substance Abuse, March 2007, at http://ccsa.ca/Resource%20Library/ccsa-011350-2007.pdf#search=rehm.

[21] Mark D. Anderson, Benjamin Hansen, and Daniel I. Rees, "Medical Marijuana Laws, Traffic Fatalities, and Alcohol Consumption," *Journal of Law and Economics*, vol.56, no. 2 (2013), pp. 333-369.This study reports that medical marijuana legalization was associated with decreased traffic fatalities. The study also noted that cannabis impairs functions such as reaction times in laboratory studies, but does not appear to impair driving in actual studies (which are summarized) because drivers engage in compensatory behavior. Under the influence of alcohol, drivers take more risks.

[22] A new study is not available, but a news article describes it. See Christopher Ingraham, "Study: Couples Who Smoke Marijuana are Less Likely to Engage in Domestic Violence," *Washington Post*, August 26, 2014. An abstract of the study, to be published in the Psychology of Addictive Behavior, can be found at http://www.ncbi.nlm.nih.gov/pubmed/25134048.

[23] National Institute of Health, National Institute of Drug Abuse, at http://www.drugabuse.gov/national-survey-druguse-health. This usage reflects the current illicit market.

[24] The smaller number is the smallest relative harm (12%) multiplied by the smaller usage rate (14%) times $30 billion. The larger number uses the largest relative harm (28%) multiplied by the larger usage rate (19%) times $30 billion. This cost could rise with legalization and lower prices, but the subsequent calculations made in this section are per unit (per ounce) and do not depend on the size of the market. If the market expands to include more casual users, the external effect per unit could decline. This estimate does not take into account the net external benefits of marijuana consumption. There are few studies that have quantified the social benefits of marijuana production (e.g., through medicinal or therapeutic methods).

[25] White House Office of National Drug Control Policy, *What America's Users Spend on Illegal Drugs: 2000-2010*, February 2014, at http://www.whitehouse.gov/sites/ default/files/ondcp/ policy-and-research/wausid_results_report.pdf. A detailed explanation of the limitations (such as underreported drug use of survey participants) of each of the data sources used in the report's analyses begins on p. 46.

[26] Most of the ADAM jurisdictions are medium to large cities within a region. See White House Office of National Drug Control Policy, *What America's Users Spend on Illegal Drugs: 2000-2010 Technical Report*, February 2014, at http://www.whitehouse.gov/sites/default/ files/ondcp/policy-and-research/wausid_technical_report.pdf.

[27] White House Office of National Drug Control Policy, *What America's Users Spend on Illegal Drugs: 2000-2010*, February 2014, p. 3, at http://www.whitehouse.gov/sites/default/ files/ondcp/policy-and-research/ wausid_results_report.pdf.

[28] These are estimates based on specific assumptions and are not the same as a range or confidence interval of the estimated size of the U.S. marijuana market. The estimates are based on total consumption, and make no distinction between underground marijuana consumption and medical marijuana that is "legal" under certain state laws. White House Office of National Drug Control Policy, *What America's Users Spend on Illegal Drugs: 2000-2010*, February 2014, pp. 58-59, at http://www.whitehouse.gov/sites/ default/files/ondcp/policy

[29] Private studies of the marijuana market find both smaller and larger effects. Jeffrey Miron and Katherine Waldock, *The Budgetary Impact of Ending Drug Prohibition*, Cato Institute, September 27, 2010, at http://www.cato.org/ publications/white-paper/budgetary-impact-ending-drug-prohibition, estimate the market at $13 billion although they acknowledge their estimates are small. Jon Gettman, "Marijuana Production in the United States," *The Bulletin of Cannabis Reform*, December 2006, http://www.drugscience.org/Archive/ bcr2/MJCropReport_2006.pdf, estimates the quantity rather than market value. At $200 to $300 per ounce, his estimates suggest a market of $106 billion to $158 billion. See also Jon Gettman, "The Supply of Marijuana to the United States," for a discussion of the method of estimating the market, at http://www.drugscience.org/Archive/bcr4/5Supply.html.

[30] CRS analysis of data from Matthew Zook, Mark Graham, and Monica Stephens, *Data Shadows of an Underground Economy: Volunteered Geographic Information and the Economic Geographies of Marijuana*, Floating Sheep Working Paper Series (FSWP001), August 30, 2011. Zook et al. reported per ounce prices for high, medium, and low quality of $377.02, $245.14, and $138.12, respectively. Observations in each category were 9,955; 5,353; and 1,194, respectively. Zook et al. removed some price-based entries from the raw data to reduce the risk of user-entry error. The data were collected across 11,860 U.S. cities. An "ounce" is equivalent to 28 grams, as some drug dealers in the underground economy use the convention of the 28 gram-ounce, instead of the precise 28.35 gram-ounce, for simplicity. Priceofweed.com does not ask users whether the marijuana was purchased through state-licensed dispensaries or through underground transactions Zook et al. also report the distribution of prices for high-quality marijuana by state. Oregon had the lowest average state price for high-quality marijuana ($256 per ounce) and Delaware had the highest ($450 per ounce).

[31] See the story of Ben Jammin, a long-time marijuana dealer, in Patrick Radden Keffe, "Buzzkill," *The New Yorker*, November 18, 2013, at http://www.newyorker.com/reporting/ 2013/11/18/131118fa_fact_keefe?currentPage=all.

[32] Steven Easton, "Legalize Marijuana for Tax Revenue," Opinion in the Business Week Debateroom, *Bloomberg Business Week*, 2009, at http://www.businessweek.com/debateroom/archives/2010/03/ legalize_marijuana_for_tax_revenue.html.

[33] The cigarette tax is $1.01 per pack of 20. For tax rates on alcohol, see CRS Report R43350, *Alcohol Excise Taxes: Current Law and Economic Analysis*, by Sean Lowry.

[34] Colorado imposes a 15% excise tax on cultivator, a 10% special sales tax, and the 2.9% standard sales tax. Washington imposes a tax on 25% at each sale point: from grower to processor, from processor to marketer, and at retail. The grower to processor tax does not apply if the grower and processor are the same.

[35] For the 9% estimate, see National Institute of Drug Abuse, "Is Marijuana Addictive?" at http://www.drugabuse.gov/ publications/research-reports/marijuana/marijuana-addictive. For an accessible discussion with differing viewpoints see, Dr. Sanjay Gupta, "Why I Changed My Mind on Weed," *CNN*, August 8, 2013, at http://www.cnn.com/2013/08/08/health/gupta-changed-mind-marijuana/; and the post of Dr. Robert Dupont at "Is Marijuana Addictive (Debate)," *Huffington Post*, September 12, 2013, at http://www.huffingtonpost.com/2012/09/04/is-marijuanaaddictive_n_1851564.html.

[36] See Hefei Wen, Jason M. Hockenberry, and Janet R. Cummings, *The Effect of Medical Marijuana Laws on Marijuana, Alcohol, and Hard Drug Use*, National Bureau of Economic Research, NBER Working Paper No. 20085, May 2014, at http://www.nber.org/papers/w20085.

[37] See Gary Becker and Kevin Murphy, "A Theory of Rational Addiction," *Journal of Political Economy*, vol. 96, no.4, 1988, pp. 675-700.

[38] David Laibson, "Golden Eggs and Hyperbolic Discounting," *Quarterly Journal of Economics*, vol. 112, no. 2, May 1997, pp. 443-477. Hyperbolic discounting means that the value of future effects falls sharply initially and then settles to a slow decline, unlike exponential discounting in which the value falls by the same proportion in every period.

[39] Jonathan Caulkins et al., *Marijuana Legalization: What Everyone Needs to Know* (Oxford: Oxford UP, 2012), p. 27. This analysis is based on the 2009 National Survey on Drug Use and Health (NSDUH).

[40] Survey evidence suggests that a marijuana tax would be regressive (like most excise taxes), because lower-income individuals are more likely to be heavier consumers of marijuana. See Figure 4.6, Beau Kilmer et al., *Before the Grand Opening: Measuring Washington State's Marijuana Market in the Last Year Before Legalized Commercial Sales*, RAND Corporation, December 2013, p. 36, at http://www.rand.org/pubs/research_ reports/RR466.html.

[41] In a competitive market, where firms do not earn profits above the amount needed to pay capital suppliers, the tax must be passed on because price must cover all costs. Even in imperfect markets, both theory and empirical evidence (such as that derived from the alcohol and tobacco markets) indicate the tax is likely to be passed forward. This issue of the pass through of excise taxes to price and references to the empirical literature are presented in in detail in CRS Report R43342, *The Medical Device Excise Tax: Economic Analysis*, by Jane G. Gravelle and Sean Lowry.

[42] Craig A. Gallet, "Can Price Get the Monkey Off Our Back? A Meta-Analysis of Illicit Drug Demand," *Health Economics*, vol. 23 (2014), pp. 55-68. See also *Altered State? Assessing How Marijuana Legalization in California Could Influence Marijuana Consumption and Public Budgets*, RAND Corporation, 2010, at http://www.rand.org/content/dam/rand/pubs/occasional_papers/2010/RAND_OP315.pdf; Kenneth W. Clements and Mert Daryal, *The Economics of Marijuana Consumption*, Economic Research Centre,

Department of Economics - The University of Western Australia, September 1999, p. 42, at http://www.drugpolicy.org/docUploads/Mari.pdf; and Henry Saffer and Frank Chaloupka, "The Demand for Illicit Drugs," *Economic Inquiry*, vol. 37, no. 3 (July 1999), pp. 401-411.

43 Following legalization, the elasticities of demand for marijuana could increase (become more price sensitive) as more casual users become part of the consumer base. However, it can be expected that the majority of demand will still be driven by heavy users, who would likely be less responsive to price changes because they may be dependent on marijuana.

44 Overall welfare could be increased, depending on the use of the tax revenue.

45 David Ruggeri, "Marijuana Price Estimates and the Price Elasticity of Demand," *International Journal of Trends in Economics, Management, & Technology (IJTEMT)*, vol. 2, no. 3 (June 2013), pp. 2321-5518.

46 Because these firms are price-takers, and are not influential enough to affect prices prevailing in the market, higher profits could signal firms to enter the industry. As quantity increases, the price will decline. Profits will converge toward normal levels, and the entry of new firms will cease.

47 Jonathan P. Caulkins, *Estimated Cost of Production for Legalized Cannabis*, RAND Corporation, July 2010, at http://www.rand.org/pubs/working_papers/WR764.html.

48 Steven Easton, "Legalize Marijuana for Tax Revenue," Opinion in the Business Week Debateroom, *Bloomberg Business Week*, 2009, at http://www.businessweek.com/debateroom/archives/2010/03/ legalize_marijuana_for_tax_revenue.html.

49 Brian Hutchinson, "Medical Marijuana Production in Canada Set for Dramatic Change," *National Post*, January 17, 2014, at http://news.nationalpost.com/2014/01/17/ medical-marijuana-production-in-canada-set-for-dramatic-change/.

50 Ibid.

51 Leafly has reviews of locations wherever recreational or medical marijuana is available (not just Colorado).

52 CRS review of prices listed for various Denver-based marijuana shops on Leafly.com was on July 23, 2014.

53 Data for Colorado, http://www.priceofweed.com/prices/United%20States/Colorado.html, visited October 27, 2014.

54 See Eric Gorski, "Reluctance of Banks Leaves Pot Shops Looking for Secure Practices," *The Denver Post*, June 15, 2014; and Alex Altman, "Colorado's New Pot Banking Law Won't Solve Cash Problems," *TIME*, June 6, 2014.

55 Beau Kilmer et al., *Altered State? Assessing How Marijuana Legalization in California Could Influence Marijuana Consumption and Public Budgets*, RAND Corporation, 2010, p. 53, at http://www.rand.org/content/dam/rand/pubs/ occasional_papers/2010/RAND_OP315.pdf.

56 Jeffrey A. Miron and Katherine Waldock, The Budgetary Impact of Ending Drug Prohibition, CATO Institute, 2010, at http://www.cato.org/pubs/wtpapers/DrugProhibitionWP.pdf. Note that only retail sales are licensed and taxed in coffee shops, as production is still illegal.

57 See Mary Wilson, "In Medical Marijuana Debate, Arguments Return to Lack of Research, Transforming Health," January 29, 2014, at http://www.transforminghealth.org/stories/2014/01/in-medical-marijuana-debate-argumentsreturn-to-lack-of-research.php; and Ryan Jaslow, "Medical Marijuana: More States Legalizing, but Scientific Evidence Lacking," *CBS News*, December 13, 2013, at http://www.cbsnews.com/news/medical-marijuana-

58 American College of Physicians, *Supporting Research into the Therapeutic Role of Marijuana*, 2008, at http://www.acponline.org/acp_policy/policies/ supporting_medmari juana_2008.pdf.

[59] For general historical context of U.S. excise tax policy, see CRS Report R43189, *Federal Excise Taxes: An Introduction and General Analysis* , by Sean Lowry.

[60] See CRS Report R40226, *P.L. 111-3: The Children's Health Insurance Program Reauthorization Act of 2009*, by Evelyne P. Baumrucker, Elicia J. Herz, and Jane G. Gravelle; and CRS Report RS22681, *The Cigarette Tax Increase to Finance SCHIP*, by Jane G. Gravelle.

[61] Assuming that the federal tax rate more than offsets any decline in price due to the effects of legalization.

[62] Most models of the potential revenue effects of a federal marijuana tax do not take into account potential exports and imports, as marijuana is still largely illegal in most overseas markets. If exports and imports were allowed, the standard tax treatment would be to tax imports of marijuana and exempt exports.

[63] Jeffrey Miron and Katherine Waldock, *The Budgetary Impact of Ending Drug Prohibition*, Cato Institute, September 27, 2010, at http://www.cato.org/publications/white-paper/budgetary-impact-ending-drug-prohibition.

[64] See CRS Report R43350, *Alcohol Excise Taxes: Current Law and Economic Analysis*, by Sean Lowry, for data.

[65] U.S. Congress, Joint Committee on Taxation, New Income and Payroll Tax Offsets to Changes in Excise Tax Revenues for 2013-2023, committee print, 113th Cong., 1st sess., February 12, 2013, JCX-5-13 (Washington: GPO, 2013).

[66] Again, this is the gain only from the excise tax, conditional on a legal market, and not from making marijuana legal, in which income taxes would increase.

[67] John Walsh, *Q&A: Legal Marijuana in Colorado and Washington*, The Brookings Institution, May 21, 2013, at http://www.brookings.edu/research/papers/2013/05/21-legal-marijuana-colorado-washington.

[68] Calculated from monthly reports at Colorado Department of Revenue, "Colorado Marijuana Tax Data," at http://www.colorado.gov/cs/Satellite/Revenue-Main/XRM/1251633259746.

[69] These estimates are based on different assumptions, and should not be considered as a range or confidence interval for what the projected national sales tax base of marijuana could be. The lower and higher estimates are based on different reported usage rates, based on age, from the NSDUH survey data. The higher estimate is based on the usage rates of 18-25 year olds and the lower estimate is based on the usage rates of those aged 26 and older. Surveys of drug habits tend to understate actual usage rates. See *Appendix C* for details.

[70] This is not to say that the ratio of medical marijuana users to recreational users is always 1:1. Based on recent tax data, it appears that the recreational and medical marijuana sales bases (before state taxes are applied) are converging. See *Appendix C* for tax revenue data from Colorado on retail and medical marijuana. Given the lower tax rates on medical marijuana, those who already have a medical marijuana registration card have little economic incentive to purchase recreational marijuana.

[71] For example, some retailers could offer "free" marijuana in combination with other goods and services. Products also tend to be more prone to theft at the retail level. In both of these situations, no tax would be paid. See Pat Oglesby, "State May Be Stuck with Second-Best Marijuana Taxes," *State Tax Notes*, June 2, 2014, pp. 539-544.

[72] The "wet" weight of a marijuana harvest is approximately four to five times its dry weight. See Jonathan P. Caulkins, *Estimated Cost of Production for Legalized Cannabis*, RAND Corporation, July 2010, p. 24, at http://www.rand.org/ content/dam/rand/pubs/working_papers/2010/RAND_WR764.pdf.

[73] For example, a tax on the "final weight" of a large, THC-infused baked good could be more than a tax based on the final weight of an individual, THC-infused lozenge, even if both products contained the same amount of THC. See Jonathan P. Caulkins et al., "High Tax States: Options for Gleaning Revenue from Legal Cannabis," *Oregon Law Review*, vol. 91 (2013), pp. 1041-1068.

[74] Pat Oglesby, "State May Be Stuck with Second-Best Marijuana Taxes," *State Tax Notes*, June 2, 2014, pp. 539-544.

[75] Jonathan P. Caulkins et al., "High Tax States: Options for Gleaning Revenue from Legal Cannabis," *Oregon Law Review*, vol. 91 (2013), pp. 1041-1068.

[76] For example, appearance or smell might affect price of dried marijuana. For baked edibles, the cost of flour, eggs, or sugar might affect the price of the final product.

[77] This is particularly the case with alcohol taxes, which have not been increased since 1993. See CRS Report R43350, *Alcohol Excise Taxes: Current Law and Economic Analysis*, by Sean Lowry.

[78] For more information, see the discussion of transition issues and floor stocks taxes in CRS Report R43189, *Federal Excise Taxes: An Introduction and General Analysis* , by Sean Lowry.

[79] See Colorado Department of Revenue, "Retail Marijuana Licensing Information," at http://www.colorado.gov/cs/ Satellite/Rev-MMJ/CBON/1251646187389.

[80] See Washington State Liquor Control Board, "FAQs on I-502," at http://lcb.wa. gov/marijuana/faqs_i-502.

[81] In the SAMSHA surveys, these respondents are divided into two age-based categories: 12-17 year olds and 18-25 year olds. According to surveys taken from 2011 to 2012, the national average of marijuana use in the past month was 7.55% for 12-17 year olds, and 18.89% for 18-25 year olds. By comparison, the national average for individuals aged 26 and older was 5.05%. See Table 3 in http://www.samhsa.gov/data/NSDUH/2k12State/Tables/ NSDUHsaeTOC2012.htm. Whole numbers are reported in: http://www. samhsa.gov/data/NSDUH/2k12State/NSDUHsae2012/NSDUHsaeStateTabs2012.htm#tab1. Some researchers have found that survey data on marijuana use understates actual use, in the range of 20% -40%, particularly among adolescents and young adults. See Jonathan P. Caulkins et al., *Marijuana Legalization: What Everyone Needs to Know* (Oxford University Press, 2012), p. 17.

[82] Eliza Gray, "New Laws Chart Course for Marijuana Legalization," *Time*, October 19, 2013, at http://nation.time.com/2013/10/19/new-laws-chart-course-for-marijuana-legalization/.

[83] See Patrick Radden Keffe, "Buzzkill," *The New Yorker*, November 18, 2013, at http://www.newyorker.com/ reporting/2013/11/18/131118fa_fact_keefe?currentPage=all. One small scale study of underground cannabis growers in Norway found that there are several financial and cultural mechanisms that tend to prevent marijuana growers from growing from small-scale to large-scale operations. Some of these mechanisms would likely not hold in a largely unregulated, commercialized market. See Eirik Hammersvik, Sveinung Sandberg, and Willy Pedersen, "Why Small-Scale Cannabis Growers Stay Small: Five Mechanisms that Prevent Small-Scale Growers from Going Large Scale," *International Journal of Drug Policy*, vol. 23 (2012), pp. 458-464.

[84] Causation between the increase in medical marijuana consumption and decrease in prescription drug overdoses has yet to be determined. See Niraj Chokshi, "Medical Marijuana States See Fewer Drug Deaths," Washington Post, p. A2, August 26, 2014.

[85] Among states where marijuana is legal for recreational or medical use, home-grow allowance laws vary based on weight or number of plants. See the National Organization for the Reform of Marijuana Laws (NORML), "State Laws," at http://norml.org/laws.

[86] See Washington State Liquor Control Board, "FAQs on I-502," at http://lcb.wa.gov/marijuana/faqs_i-502.

[87] See Pat Oglesby, "Laws to Tax Marijuana," *State Tax Notes*, January 24, 2011, pp. 251-269. Although more sophisticated, indoor plant operations are known to achieve higher yields, the point still stands that a single plant can typically supply more marijuana than a typical user consumes. Oglesby quotes estimates of annual consumption from Beau Kilmer et al., *Altered State? Assessing How Marijuana Legalization in California Could Influence Marijuana Consumption and Public Budgets*, RAND Corporation, 2010, p. 18, at http://www.rand.org/content/dam/rand/pubs/ occasional_papers/2010/RAND_OP315.pdf.

[88] Jonathan Caulkins, et al., "Design Considerations for Legalizing Cannabis: Lessons Inspired by Analysis of California's Proposition 19," *Addiction*, Society for the Study of Addiction, 2011.

[89] Evan Mills, "The Carbon Footprint of Indoor Cannabis Production," *Energy Policy*, vol. 46 (July 2012), pp. 58-67.

[90] This issue has been covered in some media outlets, such as Matt Ferner, "California County Bans Outdoor Medical Marijuana Grows," *Huffington Post*, June 4, 2014, at http://www.huffingtonpost.com/2014/06/04/lake-county-medical-marijuana_n_5441027.html. This diversion could be the result of the high price of illicit marijuana attracting growers to enter the market, though. One study found that the amount of land needed to grow enough marijuana to roughly meet current demand levels would require a relatively insignificant share of U.S. farmland (<0.01%), assuming economies of scale using outdoor production techniques. See Jonathan P. Caulkins, *Estimated Cost of Production for Legalized Cannabis*, RAND Corporation, July 2010, p.25, at http://www.rand.org/content/dam/rand/pubs/working_papers/2010/ RAND_WR764.pdf.

[91] For more information, see CRS Report R43350, *Alcohol Excise Taxes: Current Law and Economic Analysis*, by Sean Lowry.

[92] Tun-Yuan Hu, *The Liquor Tax in the United States, 1791-1947* (New York, NY: Columbia University Graduate School of Business, 1950), pp. 90-96.

[93] Pat Oglesby, "Laws to Tax Marijuana," *State Tax Notes*, January 24, 2011, pp. 251-269.

[94] Ibid.

[95] For visual examples of the RFID tagging system, see David Rosenberg, "Inside a Colorado Marijuana Dispensary," *Slate*, June 30, 2014, at http://www.slate.com/blogs/behold/ 2014/06/30/ theo_stroomer_a_look_at_medicine_man_one_of_colorado_s_largest_marijuana.html

[96] Claire Swedberg, "Colorado Readies System for Monitoring Marijuana," *RFID Journal*, December 16, 2013, at http://www.rfidjournal.com/articles/view?11283.

[97] In the domain of alcohol, for example, Treasury has issued regulations that specify exactly what kind of spirits can be labeled as "whisky." See 27 CFR 5.22.

[98] Jonathan P. Caulkins et al., "High Tax States: Options for Gleaning Revenue from Legal Cannabis," *Oregon Law Review*, vol. 91 (2013), pp. 1041-1068.

[99] For more information on hemp, see CRS Report RL32725, *Hemp as an Agricultural Commodity*, by Renée Johnson.

[100] For more comparisons on the production of hemp versus marijuana, see CRS Report RL32725, *Hemp as an Agricultural Commodity*, by Renée Johnson.

[101] The reasoning behind this prediction is that state monopolies for marijuana production or distribution cannot occur while it is still illegal at the federal level because state governments cannot force the employees of such hypothetical operations to engage in the marketing of a drug that is illegal at the federal level. See Pat Oglesby, "States May Be Stuck with Second-Best Marijuana Taxes," *State Tax Notes*, June 2, 2014, pp. 539-544.

[102] For more analysis of the option for state-run monopolies on marijuana production or retail sales, see Pat Oglesby, "States May Be Stuck with Second-Best Marijuana Taxes," *State Tax Notes*, June 2, 2014, pp. 539-544; and Jonathan P. Caulkins et al., "High Tax States: Options for Gleaning Revenue from Legal Cannabis," *Oregon Law Review*, vol. 91 (2013), pp. 1041-1068.

[103] See Vice, "Mark Kleiman on Regulating Weed: VICE Podcast 022," November 1, 2013, approximately 31:00- 33:00, YouTube.

[104] In this report, see "Taxes to Reflect External Costs" and the section titled "Spillover Effects from Alcohol Consumption" in CRS Report R43350, *Alcohol Excise Taxes: Current Law and Economic Analysis*, by Sean Lowry.

[105] See Ruth Weissenborn and David Nutt, "Popular Intoxicants: What Lessons Can be Learned from the Last 40 Years of Alcohol and Cannabis Regulation?," *Journal of Psychopharmacology*, vol. 26, no. 2 (February 2012), pp. 213-220; Gerald Thomas and Chris Davis, "Cannabis, Tobacco and Alcohol Use in Canada: Comparing Risks of Harm and Costs to Society," *Visions*, vol. 5, no. 4 (2009), p. 11; and Wayne Hall, Robin Room, and Susan Bondy, *A Comparative Appraisal of the Health and Psychological Consequences of Alcohol, Cannabis, Nicotine and Opiate Use*, World Health Organization (WHO) Project on Health Implications of Cannabis Use, August 1995, at http://www.druglibrary.org/schaffer/hemp/general/who-index.htm. For a comparison of the social costs of alcohol and tobacco see Willard G. Manning et al., *The Costs of Poor Health Habits* (Cambridge, MA: Harvard University Press, 1991).

[106] For a summary of some of these studies, most of which analyze trends in youth consumption, see Table 15 in Kenneth W. Clements and Mert Daryal, *The Economics of Marijuana Consumption*, Economic Research Centre, Department of Economics - The University of Western Australia, September 1999, p. 42, at http://www.drugpolicy.org/docUploads/Mari.pdf. For a study on the effects of U.S. medical marijuana laws (MMLs) on alcohol consumption, see Hefei Wen, Jason M. Hockenberry, and Janet R. Cummings, *The Effect of Medical Marijuana Laws on Marijuana, Alcohol, and Hard Drug Use*, National Bureau of Economic Reseach, NBER Working Paper No. 20085, May 2014, at http://www.nber.org/papers/w20085. Wen et al. find that among those aged 21 and older, MMLs increased the frequency of binge drinking by 6%-9%, but MMLs did not affect drinking behavior among those 12-20 years old.

[107] For a more detailed discussion of the general shortcomings of this body of research, see Jonathan P. Caulkins et al., *Marijuana Legalization: What Everyone Needs to Know* (Oxford University Press, 2012), pp. 133-135.

[108] Gardiner Harris, "Researchers Find Study of Medical Marijuana Discouraged," *New York Times*, January 18, 2010, at http://www.nytimes.com/2010/01/ 19/health/policy/19marijuana.html.

[109] Most researchers argue that alcohol excise tax rates are set below the economically efficient level to compensate for social costs. One estimate finds the combined federal, state, and local taxes between 25 cents and 27 cents (in 2011 dollars) per ounce of pure alcohol compared with the external cost of 97 cents per ounce. See CRS Report R43350, *Alcohol Excise Taxes: Current Law and Economic Analysis*, by Sean Lowry.

[110] Caulkins et al. (2012), pp. 131-132. Also see Hefei Wen, Jason M. Hockenberry, and Janet R. Cummings, *The Effect of Medical Marijuana Laws on Marijuana, Alcohol, and Hard Drug Use*, National Bureau of Economic Reseach, NBER Working Paper No. 20085, May 2014, at http://www.nber.org/papers/w20085. Wen et al. find that MMLs had no discernible impact on hard drug use in either youth or adults in U.S. states that legalized marijuana for medical purposes.

[111] See Figure 4.7 in Beau Kilmer et al., *Before the Grand Opening: Measuring Washington State's Marijuana Market in the Last Year Before Legalized Commercial Sales*, RAND Corporation, December 2013, p. 37, at http://www.rand.org/pubs/research_reports/RR466.html.

[112] Giovanni Battistella et al., "Weed or Wheel! fMRI, Behavioural, and Toxicological Investigations of How Cannabis Smoking Affects Skills Necessary for Driving," *PLoS ONE*, vol. 8, no. 1 (2013); and Rebecca L. Hartman and Marilyn A. Huestis, "Cannabis Effects on Driving Skills," *Clinical Chemistry*, vol. 59, no. 3 (December 2012), pp. 478-492.

[113] Guohua Li, Joanne E. Brady, and Qixuan Chen, "Drug Use and Fatal Motor Vehicle Crashes: A Case-Control Study," *Accident Analysis and Prevention*, vol. 60 (2013), pp. 205-210. For data analysis, see Joanne E. Brady and Guohua Li, "Prevalence of Alcohol and Other Drugs in Fatally Injured Drivers," *Addiction*, vol. 108, no. 1 (January 2013), pp. 104-114; and Amelia M. Arria et al., "Substance-Related Traffic-Risk Behaviors among College Students," *Drug and Alcohol Dependence*, vol. 118, no. 2-3 (November 2011), pp. 306-312.

[114] Joanne E. Brady and Guohua Li, "Trends in Alcohol and Other Drugs Detected in Fatally Injured Drivers in the United States, 1999-2010," *American Journal of Epidemiology*, vol. 179, no. 6 (2014), pp. 692-699.

[115] Jeffrey A. Miron, *The Budgetary Implications of Marijuana Prohibition*, Marijuana Policy Project, June 2005, at http://www.prohibitioncosts.org/mironreport/.

[116] For specific critiques of Miron's study, see Jonathan P. Caulkins et al., "What are the Pros and Cons of Legalization Generally?" in *Marijuana Legalization: What Everyone Needs to Know* (Oxford: Oxford University Press, 2012), pp. 129-130.

[117] Eric L. Sevigny and Jonathan P. Caulkins, "Kingpins or Mules: An Analysis of Drug Offenders Incarcerated in Federal and State Prisons," *Criminology and Public Policy*, vol. 3, no. 3 (July 2004), pp. 401-434. Other convictions that involved marijuana possession and another offense (e.g., robbery) could still result in prison time.

[118] See Figure A in U.S. Sentencing Commission, *2013 Sourcebook of Federal Sentencing Statistics*, http://www.ussc.gov/research-and-publications/annual-reports-sourcebooks/2013/sourcebook-2013; and CRS Report R42937, *The Federal Prison Population Buildup: Overview, Policy Changes, Issues, and Options*, by Nathan James.

[119] According to Department of Justice data, nearly 99% of sentenced drug offenders are sent to federal prison for trafficking offenses. For analysis of the most recent data, see CRS Report R42937, *The Federal Prison Population Buildup: Overview, Policy Changes, Issues, and Options*, by Nathan James.

[120] See Figure A in U.S. Sentencing Commission, *2013 Sourcebook of Federal Sentencing Statistics*, http://www.ussc.gov/research-and-publications/annual-reports-sourcebooks/2013/sourcebook-2013.

[121] Another factor that could affect federal prison populations is any changes to federal sentencing guidelines for drug trafficking. For more information, see CRS Report WSLG814, *Lower Drug Trafficking Penalties, Sentencing Commission Proposes*, by Charles Doyle.

[122] Jonathan P. Caulkins et al., "What are the Pros and Cons of Legalization Generally?" in *Marijuana Legalization: What Everyone Needs to Know* (Oxford: Oxford University Press, 2012), pp. 129-130.

[123] Caulkins et al. (2012), p. 131.

[124] For more legal analysis, see CRS Report WSLG1101, *Federal Taxation of Marijuana Sellers*, by Erika K. Lunder.

[125] Katy Steinmetz, "Christian Pot Dispensary Takes on IRS," *TIME*, February 19, 2014, at http://time.com/8764/medical-marijuana-legalization-pot-christian-canna-care-lanette-davies/.

126 "Medical Marijuana Dispensary Takes on IRS over What It Calls 'Punitive' Taxes," *Washington Post*, February 23, 2014, at http://www.washingtonpost.com/politics/medical-marijuana-dispensary-takes-on-irs-over-what-it-callspunitive-taxes/2014/02/23/25fa6458-9cd3-11e3-ad71-e03637a299c0_story.html.

[127] With 35% being the top, marginal tax bracket for corporations and 39.6% being the top, marginal tax bracket for individuals under the federal income tax code.

[128] Colorado imposes a sales tax of 10% and an excise tax of 15% on retail marijuana sales, in addition to a general 2.9% state sales tax and any local sales taxes. See State of Colorado Department of Revenue, "Retail Marijuana Return Filing Overview," January 29-31, 2014, at http://www.colorado.gov/cms/forms/dor-tax/ RetailMarijuanaReturnFiling OverviewJan2014.pdf. The state of Washington, which will allow recreational marijuana sales later in 2014, will impose an excise tax of 25% on the sales price of marijuana within an established, state-distribution system.

[129] It is more difficult to calculate the state tax base using collections data from 15% retail medical tax because this tax is calculated on state-set average prices for various categories of marijuana.

[130] The exact figure is $2,940,346.

[131] Colorado Department of Revenue, "Colorado Marijuana Tax Data," at https://www.colorado.gov/pacific/revenue/ colorado-marijuana-tax-data.

[132] The exact calculations result in tax base calculations of $29,403,460 and $30,583,276, respectively.

[133] The exact calculation is $29,993,368.

[134] The lower and higher estimates are based on different reported usage rates, based on age, from the NSDUH survey data. The higher estimate is based on the usage rates of 18-25 year olds and the lower estimate is based on the usage rates of 26+ year olds. Surveys of drug habits tend to understate actual usage rates. These estimates are based on different assumptions, and they should not be considered as a range or confidence interval for what the projected national sales tax base of marijuana could be.

[135] This calculation is based on $886,915 collected In September 2014 from the 2.9% general sales tax. See Colorado Department of Revenue, "Colorado Marijuana Tax Data," at https://www.colorado.gov/pacific/revenue/coloradomarijuana-tax-data.

[136] Calculations based on $9.1 million in reported tax collections during FY2013. See Colorado Department of Revenue, "Colorado Medical Marijuana Dispensaries, Retail Sales and State Tax by County, Fourth Quarter, FY2012- 13," at http://www.colorado.gov/cs/Satellite?c=Document_C&childpagename=RevenueMain%2FDocument_C%2FXRMAddLink&cid=1251647950747&pagename=XRMWrapper.

[137] Medical marijuana patient data is available at Marijuana Policy Project, "Medical Marijuana Patient Numbers," at http://www.mpp.org/states/medical-marijuana-patient.html. Some states do not disclose their number of medical marijuana patients, doctors, or caregivers.

INDEX

A

B

C

D

E

F

G

H

I

J

L

Q

R

S

T

U

V

W

Y